JOHN ROBSHAW PRINTS

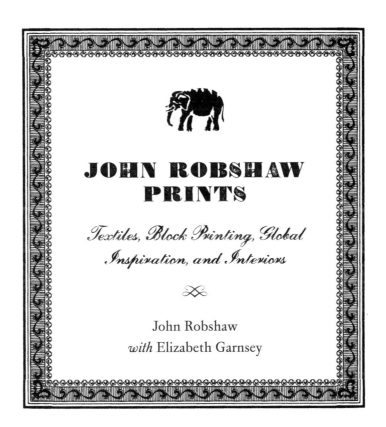

JOHN ROBSHAW PRINTS

Textiles, Block Printing, Global Inspiration, and Interiors

✕

John Robshaw

with Elizabeth Garnsey

CHRONICLE BOOKS

SAN FRANCISCO

Library of Congress Cataloging-in-Publication Data:

Robshaw, John.

John Robshaw prints : textiles, block printing, global inspiration, and interiors /

John Robshaw with Elizabeth Garnsey.

p. cm.

Includes bibliographical references.

ISBN 978-1-4521-0505-5

1. Textile design. 2. Textile printing. 3. Textile fabrics in interior decoration.

I. Garnsey, Elizabeth, 1970– II. Title.

NK8806.R63 2012

746.6092—dc23

2011046320

Manufactured in China

Designed by Sarah Caplan

Text on page 7 courtesy of the Burchfield Penney Art Center,

Charles E. Burchfield Archives.

1 3 5 7 9 10 8 6 4 2

Chronicle Books LLC

680 Second Street

San Francisco, California 94107

www.chroniclebooks.com

CONTENTS

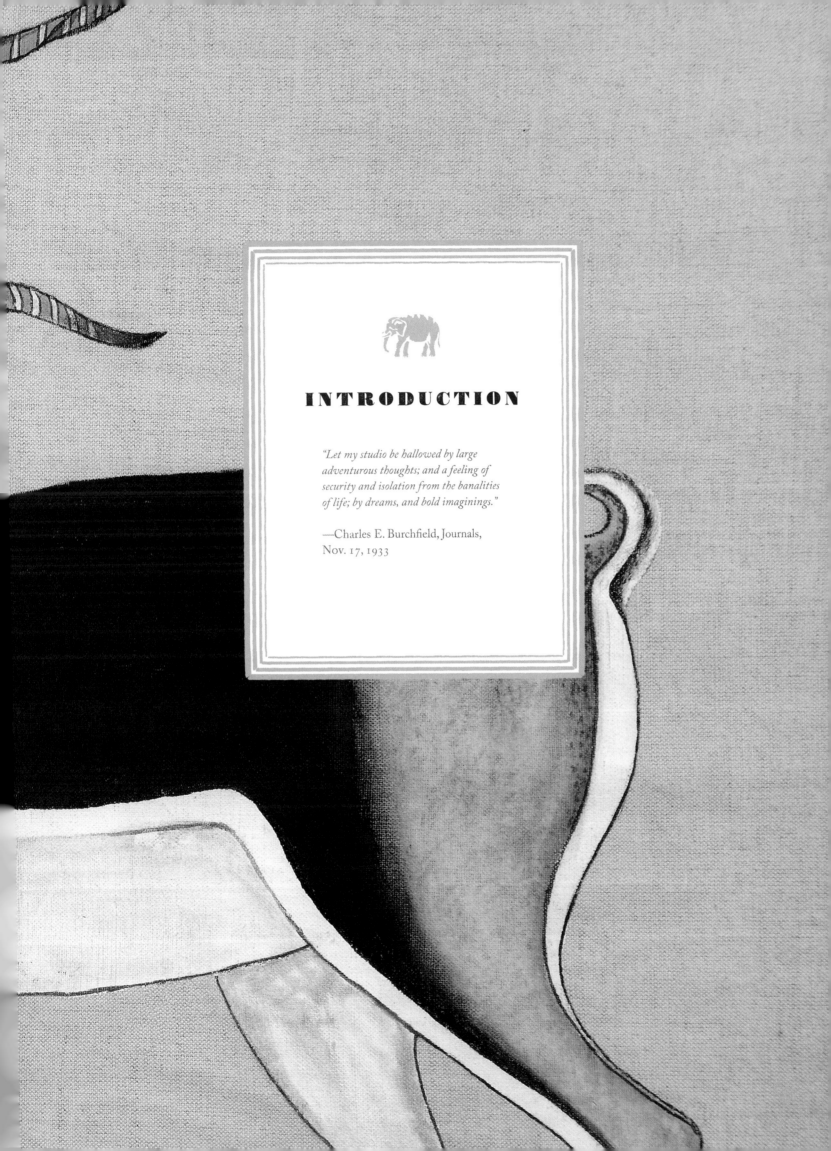

INTRODUCTION

"Let my studio be hallowed by large adventurous thoughts; and a feeling of security and isolation from the banalities of life; by dreams, and bold imaginings."

—Charles E. Burchfield, Journals, Nov. 17, 1933

A typical dispatch from one of John Robshaw's travels goes like this: "Dear Dears, Have been run over by boys racing donkeys. Fear it is omen. Watching belly dancers with dinner. Think office should take it up as a hobby. Colleen and Al will excel. Happy Hanukkuh Merry Xmas etc. —John."

This was a postcard from Jordan, addressed to "Robshaw Gang," otherwise known as the staff at John's showroom in New York City's Garment District. Ever the intrepid traveler, John has a knack for seizing a detail and making a whole scene of it. He has a way of bringing others to where he has been, whether through a postcard or through a pillow, but chances are, other people who go to places he's been would never be able to capture a scene quite the way he can.

I first met John in 1999, when I was researching a story for *Travel + Leisure* magazine about globe-trotting designers who work abroad with indigenous artisans. He was just starting out in his textiles business. His hand-block-printed fabrics (some by his own hand) were being sold out of other people's showrooms (Charles Jacobsen in Los Angeles, Kevin Jacobs in New York), and he was a secret source for Calvin Klein and Ralph Lauren.

Before I had actually met John face-to-face, I was presented with an eight-inch, rubber band–bound stack of photographs he had taken on his most recent trip to India.

There were pictures of camels all dressed up for festivals, and of yards upon yards of multicolored, freshly dyed fabrics hanging over wooden scaffolds to dry, blowing in the breeze. There were shots of blue-stained hands (indigo dyers) wringing out cotton fabrics and Indians toiling away over boiling vats of dark dye, and someone had wrested the camera to take one of John, sitting in the courtyard of the Hotel Diggi Palace, his home base in Jaipur to this day. In the picture, his bare feet were stretched out in front of him as he sat in a garden chair, and he wore a block-printed button-down shirt (no doubt one he'd printed himself), with pants rolled up at the ankle. The easy smile on his face said he was home, a master of his domain.

It turns out that, in a real way, he was. As we have become friends over the years in New York, I see John first and foremost as a traveler, a seeker, a happy foreigner who is at his most restless in his native land.

With John, the challenge of piecing together my short *Travel + Leisure* article was to zero in on just one of his many experiences of traveling to work with local artists. He had worked alongside textile makers in Peru, Bolivia, Zimbabwe, Cambodia, Thailand, Laos, India, and beyond. He had gone often as a consultant with Aid to Artisans, an organization that sends established designers and artists to various countries where they help people develop their indigenous crafts from cottage industries into viable businesses that can grow to support whole populations.

John has the kind of outlook that made him a perfect fit for such missions. He is fearless, open to any kind of adventure, hungry to learn from others, and completely at ease in strange places where he may not be able to speak the language, digest the food, or outrun the donkeys. Some words the poet and essayist Kenneth Rexroth penned about Marco Polo could be applied to John Robshaw as well: "What is most impressive about Marco Polo is not that he finds men in distant lands strange and their ways outlandish, but that he does not." Both men have the "tolerance that comes from thinking of one

Fatehpur Sikri, the 1571 Mughal Empire's capital city.

world linked together by caravan journeys and sea voyages, three years or more long; the tremendous civilizing force of business as business in the face of the most anomalous customs."

In spite of the many obstacles to doing business in places like India or Thailand or Indonesia—monsoons and camel festivals, harvests and typhoid attacks—John has figured out how to go with the flow when the "flow" may be more like a spewing fire hydrant, or an empty well. He has spent years cultivating a sense of camaraderie among the people he has met and worked with. Unfazed by cultural divides, John makes friends with locals in these far-flung places he loves, earning their trust—and appealing to their sense of humor—by coming alongside them first as their apprentice, to watch, learn, mess up, try new things, and then developing as an artist by blending their shared expertise with his own original ideas.

Finally choosing to base his production in India, John persisted through years of trial and error to find the most skilled artisans to work with among the sea of choices in a country where seemingly everyone is an artisan and textile making is the national pastime. But his sharp eye for beauty and originality helped John come upon just the right block carvers, dye masters, and printers, whom he convinced to apply their ancient heritage and traditional skills to making his unfamiliar prints and modernized art-meets-textile creations. These artisans had to be highly skilled and at the same time willing to let the process show. In other words, they had to set aside block printing's typically rigid, perfectionistic standards and be a little more like John: willing to try new things, free and fluid, open to the random missteps and surprises that make life so much more interesting.

In this book, John explores his commitment as an artist to the process behind his product. He shares the extraordinary path, from Buffalo to Beijing, from Java to Jaipur, that has shaped and formed him as the insatiable wandering seeker of an artist that he is. In a variety of ways when he's on the road,

TOP: Egypt's White Desert. BOTTOM: An ancient Indian fort.

John reminds himself "that life is a sloppy, chaotic patchwork that amazingly comes together." In a letter home from Calcutta, he says he had this thought "while dodging traffic, narrowly avoiding being slammed by a taxi just after reading the headline 'Kaziranga Tiger Shot Dead While Feeding on Forest Dweller.'"

Nothing much rattles the cage of this fellow, whose escapades range from the momentous to the absurd. As an art student in China in 1989, John had a brush with destiny, getting kicked out of Tiananmen Square when the violent government crackdowns began. He has narrowly escaped an attack by a camel in heat while horseback riding to a festival in Pushkar, India. He has been advised by a sidewalk seer's fortune-telling rabbit, "Hey you! Inventor! A very important action going to change your life! You must be careful and part!"

Never precious or pretentious, never snobby or cynical, John maintains a child's sense of wonder and adventure. He thrills at continuing to discover the best of the world's most beautiful textile-making traditions, and reveres the human hands that carry them forward. And John will take his design inspirations from everywhere: spinning prayer wheels in Tibet, Jain temple pilgrims mounting miles of marble steps in bare feet, Kathmandu juggernauts bearing statues of deities with beer issuing from their mouths, intricate carvings in the stone walls of a monastery, bright blue peacocks squawking in a hotel garden, the stripes of an unraveled turban, stories of leopards creeping into villages to pounce on goats. All of these images, and more, weave their way into the weft and warp of John Robshaw Textiles, as this book so beautifully illustrates. In the words of the artist himself, "Please enjoy the festival."

—Elizabeth Garnsey

OPPOSITE: Wedding musicians trumpet a new line.

Super cook, Mellous & camels,
Horses, cows & Village guys.
Horse traders a disreputable lot!

TEXTILE PRINTING

"You must know that the pepper-trees are cultivated, being regularly planted and watered; and the pepper is gathered in the months of May, June, and July. They have also abundance of very fine indigo. This is made of a certain herb which is gathered, and is put into great vessels upon which they pour water and then leave it till the whole of the plant is decomposed. They then put this liquid in the sun, which is tremendously hot there, so that it boils and coagulates, and becomes such as we see it."

—Marco Polo, THE TRAVELS OF MARCO POLO, translated by Henry Yule

If they could, every one of my textiles would pipe up with a story. And not just a single story, but an interwoven narrative about a particular trip to a distant country, and the people I meet there, the ideas they inspire, and the techniques they are generous enough to teach me. Wherever I travel, whether to India or Thailand, Indonesia or Nepal, I draw from the visual art and music and languages I hear, as much as from the overgrown exotic gardens and ancient temples I see, and the religious festivals and the Bollywood mayhem of the street life I negotiate, to make new prints. But it is the traditional printing methods I've learned along the way that have unleashed countless new ideas. They are what have opened up unexpected new directions for me as I have grown as an artist and designer; I've just stumbled in, the way local taxicabs careen left or right—or seemingly both at the same time—but you can't predict the direction, so you just have to jump into the void.

My travels have introduced me to dozens of indigenous printing techniques, but a few have become central to my collections over the years. Block printing became my teacher and my muse, and my temperamental mistress. I was drawn to it the first time I saw it done in India, and I fell in love with it—and with India, too. If my personality were an art form, I would be block printing. The rhythm and method allow for all

OPPOSITE: Block carvers in Sanganer. ABOVE: Note how delicately the printer lines up the block before he stamps.

kinds of free-form ideas and random action. Any missteps or confusion can become instead an innovation, a new style. The beauty of block printing's exactitude is equal to the fun of its malleability. Many of the photos in this chapter provide a glimpse into the expertise of the printers and artisans with whom I work in India, along with a step-by-step illustration of how block printing gets done.

I am indebted to all of my friends in India whom I have had the pleasure (and pain, at times) to work with over the years and to learn from and grow with. To say the least, it has not always been easy—though I have enjoyed our tussles, brawls, and near misses. On the other hand, I have been on the receiving end of their amazing hospitality, their insights, and their support as partners and friends.

A few other techniques I incorporate into my collections but don't rely on, because of technical challenges, are the batiking I learned in Yogyakarta, Indonesia; mud printing with natural indigo, which I attempted in Bagru, India; and ikat weaving in Isaan, Thailand, where I merely watched, mesmerized, as the looms swayed back and forth. But elements of all of these, along with block printing, are what come together to form my hybrid, eccentric designs that are at once ancient and modern, time-honored and original—for better or for worse!

Block Printing

Some scholars believe block printing originated in India as early as 3000 B.C.E., but no actual textiles or blocks that old have survived. Printed textiles were used in parts of the Caucasus Mountains around 2000 B.C.E. And Herodotus (450 B.C.E.) makes reference in his histories to peoples from the same region who painted animal figures on their clothing, while Strabo, who lived from 63 B.C.E. to 20 C.E. in what is now Turkey, documents Indian printed textiles. And in the first century C.E.,

OPPOSITE: A quilt in progress being stamped with my "Hedge" print, Spring 2010.

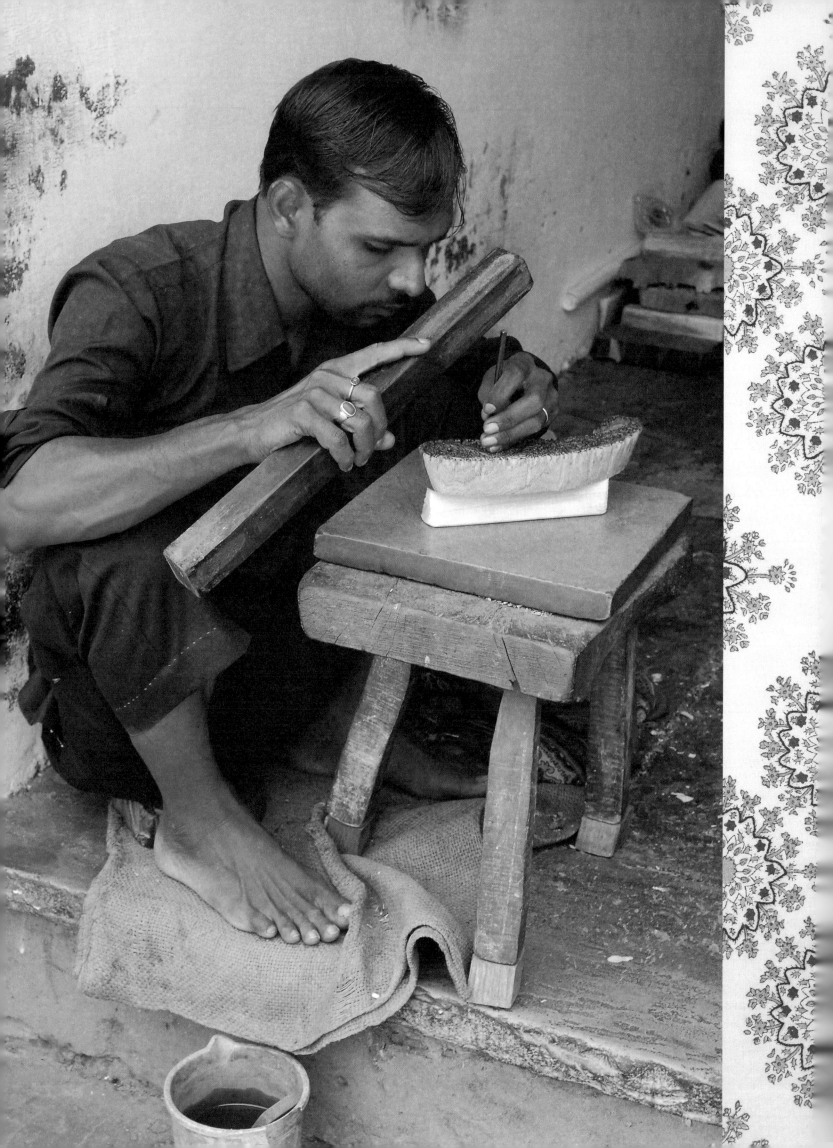

Pliny the Elder alludes to the painting and dyeing of textiles. Archeologists in Egypt uncovered the earliest known block-printed fabric, a fourth-century child's tunic in white linen, stamped with blue star-shaped designs in a diamond pattern.

But many scholars believe it was in India where the practice of printing fabrics was perfected, as early as the twelfth century, and it was Indian craftsmen who elevated it to the world-renowned art form it became by about the seventeenth century. That was when families of artisans called *chhipas* (literally, people who stamp or print) settled in the town of Bagru, about thirty-five kilometers east of Jaipur. There, by the river Sanjaria, generation after generation perfected and perpetuated the art of block printing; in many cases, to this day, Bagru printers have managed to preserve the use of natural dyes in spite of enormous commercial pressure to change to synthetics. Many of the *chhipas*, who are all Hindu and whose families have practiced this art for generations, revere traditional materials and methods and consider their work a form of worship.

I do most of my block printing in the town of Sanganer (a suburb of Jaipur), which, like Bagru, has been home to a community of printers for centuries. During the eighteenth century, the artisans streamlined their designs to appeal to a wider market. Demand among royalty for garb to wear in festivals and court processions boosted domestic trade, and the work of the Sanganeri craftspeople eventually expanded into an international market as one of the East India Company's major exports. Today, more than 150 block-printing workshops exist in Sanganer, and almost twenty thousand people there depend on the craft for their livelihood.

From the mixing of dyes and the carving of wooden blocks to the technique of stamping the fabric, the skill of the Indian artisan is without parallel in the world of block printing. Natural dye colors are derived from sources such as old iron camel or horseshoes soaked in water for black dye; alum, gum paste, or pomegranate rind for red dye; and madder root

OPPOSITE: Chipping away at a block for my "Darter" print.

(straw) or turmeric for yellow dye. Some of these colors hold sacred symbolic significance, which you might have guessed if you've ever seen a blue-faced statue of Lord Krishna, or a saffron-cloaked Buddhist monk, or a yellow-robed yogi.

To ready the printing station, the printer cushions the table with two dozen layers of jute, then pins down six or eight layers of thin cotton fabric. The layers cushion the blocks (extending their wear) and assure the dyes will be absorbed evenly. In the print unit are several tables, each as wide as the printer can reach, and as long as a dozen feet. There's a mellow rhythm to the way the printers move past each other, back and forth, performing the various steps—pinning, setting dye trays, brushing off blocks to prepare them for fresh dye. The patterns unfold in layers, slowly but surely, with each lap the printer takes up and down his table.

THE PRINTER'S PACE

The printers work slowly and methodically in the heat of the day. They ride their bikes to the shop and ride them home for lunch; then they lie around on the tables, relaxing in the swelter upon returning before the printing starts again. There is the constant blare of Bollywood music in the background. On top of that, you hear the repeated rhythm of printing and you see the progress as the print grows and comes to life, how it unfolds as one block connects to the other blocks to create a larger motif. The pattern grows into an orb and then into a medallion. . . . Then the medallion grows and repeats as negative space becomes positive space. Once the cloth has been printed, it is unpinned from the table, and taken—by two men, so it won't get smudged—down to hang on the line or up on the roof to dry in the sun. The blocks are left in haphazard rows under the printing tables. But somehow the printers can always find the blocks they need among the dusty piles.

OPPOSITE: Aligning the block to stamp my "Champa Vista" print. The printing cloth under the fabric being printed bears the residue of earlier designs.

The dye master is a key character in any workshop. If he disappears for a wedding or gets sick, the whole workshop grinds to a halt. And some of the biggest rows I have seen in workshops are sparked by incidents with dye masters and some miscalculation in colors. Like a mad scientist, the dye master mixes his plant powders or pigments in plastic buckets, stirring quickly and peering intensely into the buckets to see the colors, adding a pinch of this or that. As he mixes the dyes, he dabs them on small pieces of cotton fabric, letting them dry to assess the true color. Once the dyes are just right, the color master passes off the buckets to printers, who pour the dyes into trays, which are then loaded onto wheeled trolleys.

The trays are more than simple pans—they are more like ink pads. They are usually made of wood, and are fitted with a layer of bamboo or metal mesh in the bottom to keep them shallow enough not to overload the stamps with dye when they are dipped. A layer or two of cotton over the mesh, and a final thin layer of gauze over the cotton, prevent lumps and blobs from forming in the dye.

The printer makes a couple of test stamps before starting in on the actual yardage. These first random stamps, one on top of another on the layers of padding cloth, make beautifully random designs and are one of my favorite parts of block printing. They evoke the passage of time, the hand of each printer who worked at this table, and the layers of colors and ideas that were tried on the way to a final design.

Once everything is set up, printers take up their blocks for the first dip into the dye, then make a swift move toward the cloth-covered table. They position the block precisely and gently on the fabric and strike it twice or three times in a rhythmic drumming motion with the heel of their hand to make the imprint; then it's back to the dye cart for more color. The palm of a printer's hand feels like that of a prize fighter, calloused from repeating this process over and over again, the spacing often guided only by his experienced eye and patient expertise.

OPPOSITE, CLOCKWISE FROM TOP: Dye master mixing color; pigment portions are weighed on a scale; a used piece of mesh leans between a bucket of silver dye and a tray of gold dye that was used for the "Darter" line.

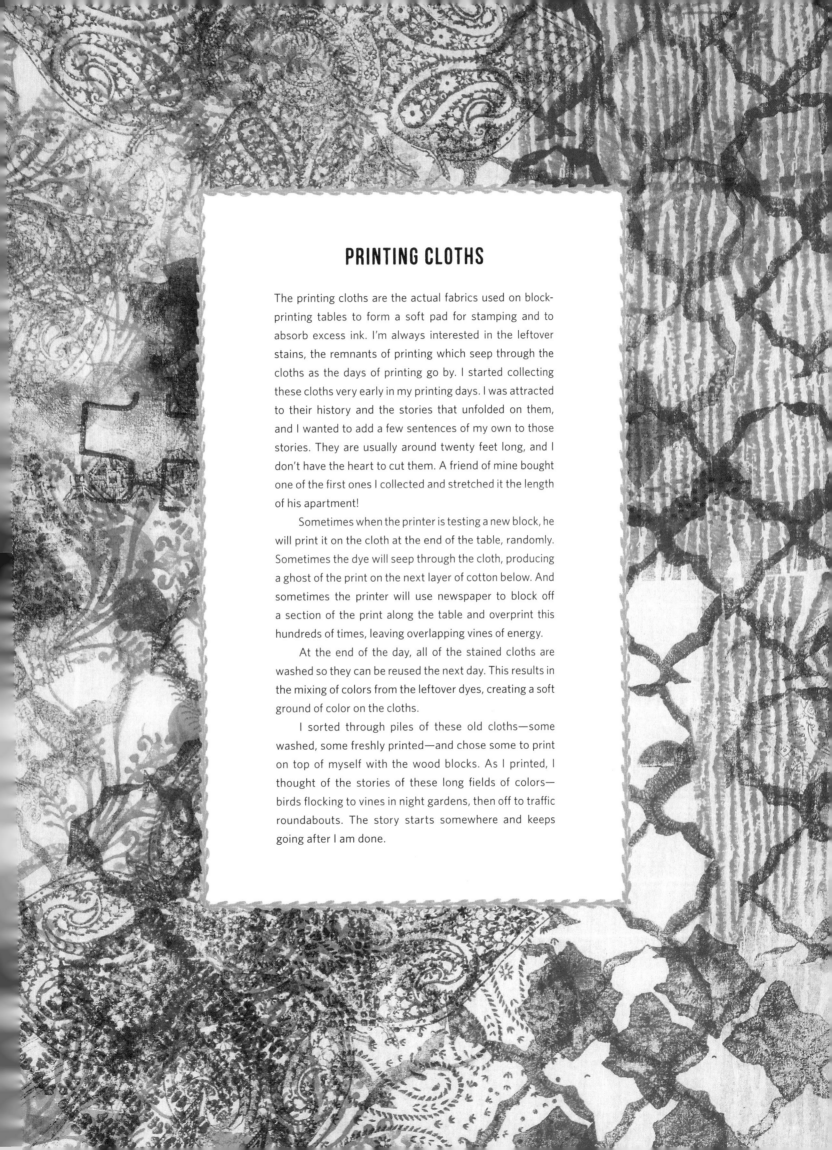

PRINTING CLOTHS

The printing cloths are the actual fabrics used on block-printing tables to form a soft pad for stamping and to absorb excess ink. I'm always interested in the leftover stains, the remnants of printing which seep through the cloths as the days of printing go by. I started collecting these cloths very early in my printing days. I was attracted to their history and the stories that unfolded on them, and I wanted to add a few sentences of my own to those stories. They are usually around twenty feet long, and I don't have the heart to cut them. A friend of mine bought one of the first ones I collected and stretched it the length of his apartment!

Sometimes when the printer is testing a new block, he will print it on the cloth at the end of the table, randomly. Sometimes the dye will seep through the cloth, producing a ghost of the print on the next layer of cotton below. And sometimes the printer will use newspaper to block off a section of the print along the table and overprint this hundreds of times, leaving overlapping vines of energy.

At the end of the day, all of the stained cloths are washed so they can be reused the next day. This results in the mixing of colors from the leftover dyes, creating a soft ground of color on the cloths.

I sorted through piles of these old cloths—some washed, some freshly printed—and chose some to print on top of myself with the wood blocks. As I printed, I thought of the stories of these long fields of colors—birds flocking to vines in night gardens, then off to traffic roundabouts. The story starts somewhere and keeps going after I am done.

Block Printing Step By Step

BLOCK CARVING

Block carving is its own art, and the craftspeople who make block carvings are very specialized. The best blocks come from knotless, smooth cross sections of teak tree trunks. The wood is soaked in oil sometimes for up to two weeks, sanded smooth, and then whitened with chalk. The carvers trace designs onto the surface and then, using only hammer and chisel and a delicate touch, whittle patterns into the wood (see above). A well-made block can last through printing anywhere from 1,000 to 1,500 meters of fabric before its fine edges wear down. For especially fine designs, some blocks are made of brass or copper, with crisp-edged strips that are bent on a tree trunk and affixed to a base.

ORIGINAL STAMP

While block printing is an ancient art of precision, I like my printers to leave an original stamp, so to speak, on their work. Sometimes they have a laugh or literally scratch their heads over the atypical designs I devise for them to create. I will print some of the patterns to show them how I want it, or guide their hands as they print to show them a certain order I want them to print in. I aim for a fusion of the techniques that have been used for centuries with a modern sensibility and my own taste in patterns, forms, and rhythms that I think will impact the final design. To me, how a thing is made is as important as what it finally becomes, so the progression of how the print is stamped is essential. I am going not as much for perfection as I am for personality.

CARVING A BLOCK

Above: A new block ready for stamping. This one was used for my "Darter" print. *Opposite:* A new design is first traced onto the wood with black pencil. Then it's "punched" into the wood so a carver can refine it with a chisel. Detailed carving of a new block can take many hours or a couple of days to complete.

PREPARATIONS

Above: Several layers of base fabric are pinned to the printing table, which creates a cushion effect so dyes can be absorbed better and more evenly. These printing layers are washed thoroughly between printings, but they become so stained that their history in the workshop comes through. *Opposite:* This yardage of dark fabric will be printed with a bright metallic dye. It is pinned down every six to ten inches on top of the base cloths to keep it in place.

THE DYE

Above: A dye mixer pours color into a tray, into the mesh screen and linen layers that will keep the color from forming lumps while stamps are repeatedly dipped into it. *Opposite, clockwise from top:* White-on-blue "Cobalt" line being stamped; used trays of gold, pink, and blue; the stamping pad is saturated with color, then wrung out in preparation for block printing.

PRINTING

Opposite, top right: My take on a classic print was destined for a line of pillows I called Gomati Madder. Gomati is a tributary of the Ganges River, and the madder root has been an important source of red dye for over 5,000 years around the world, from Egypt to India to Scandinavia. The metallic dye is made up of copper and gold. *Opposite, top left and bottom:* "Darter" print in progress. *Above:* Printing a "Blossom" pillow.

Opposite: A fine-lined block print such as the Gomati Madder requires some exacting skills; to apply the dye evenly, the printer lines up the block with his fingers, then gives it a "one-two" punch with the heel of each hand. *Above:* The printer drags a small spatula-like tool through a tray to maintain an even layer of dye and to ensure the blocks will be properly inked for each repetition on the cloth.

DISCHARGE PRINTING

Above and opposite: On fabrics with a dark base color, discharge printing is done using a bleach paste, which takes the base color back to white. Here the printer carefully lines up the block along the edges first, to make sure the print is balanced within the pillow.

MANEUVERING THE FABRIC

Opposite: It takes two people to adjust a large cloth and to avoid smudging the stamps in the middle of a job.

Above: A printed piece is hung carefully and left to dry for several hours.

DISCHARGING

Discharging is a process used to set the dye into the fabric after a print has dried completely. *Above:* A dry, newly printed cloth is rolled up in padded cloths and placed into a large steamer before it is hung up to dry in the sun. *Opposite, clockwise from top left:* Pillow prints being rolled up for discharging; a roll is placed into the steamer; a discharged cloth about to be hung up to dry; unrolling padded cloths after steaming.

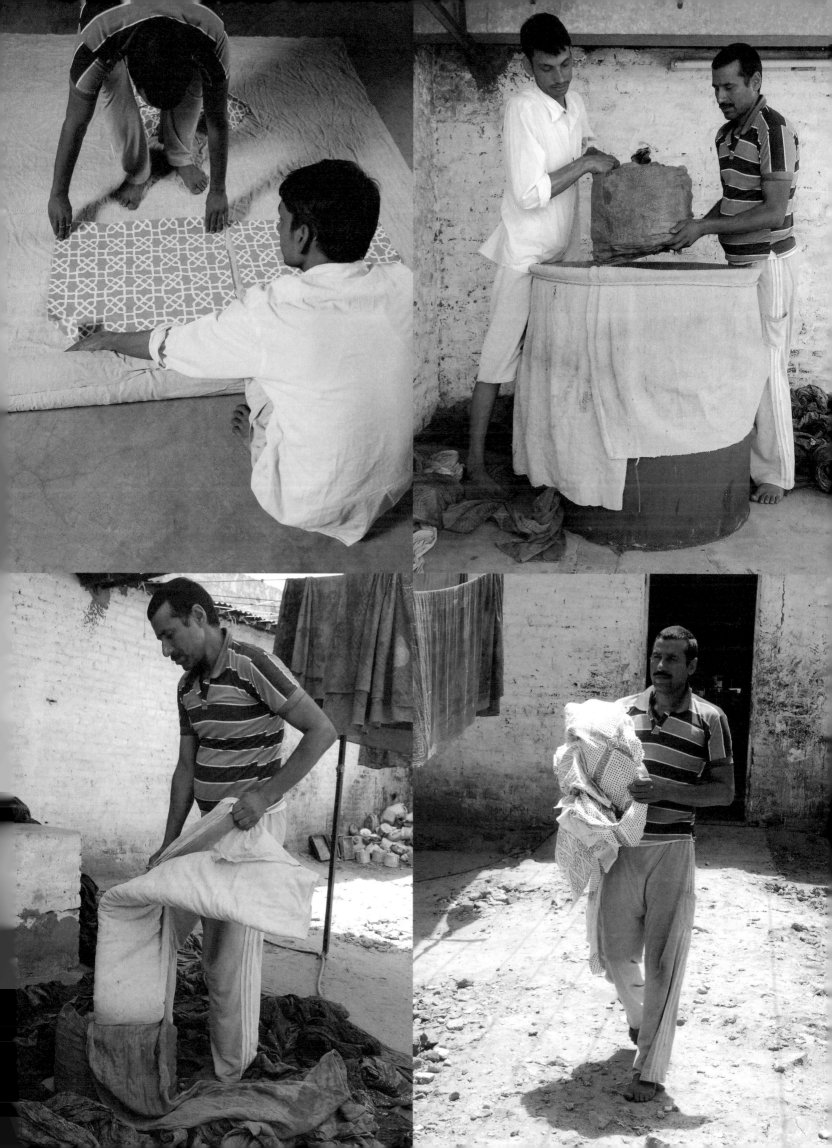

Opposite and above: After steaming, there is more soaking, washing, and scrubbing to remove excess dye before hanging final prints to dry. Thicker fabrics especially need to be scrubbed so excess dye won't bleed.

Above: A happy gang of printers outside the workshop. *Opposite, clockwise from top left:* Showcasing the "Han" block used for clay resist; wielding the "Gomati Madder" block; a mosaic pillowcase, ready to go; displaying the "Darter" block.

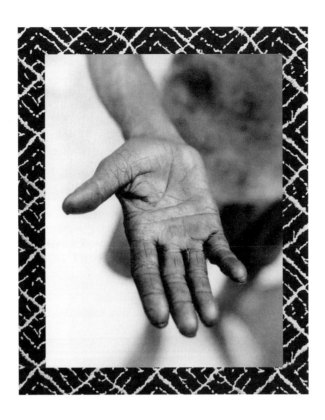

Indigo

Indigo has been used around the world for centuries and was once considered very dear. It was a color reserved for both royal and religious vestments, and was also used as a hair dye and body paint (used the way henna is now) and valued as a medicine for its antiseptic and anti-inflammatory properties. India is the oldest indigo-dye producer in the world; as early as the Greco-Roman era, India kept all of Europe supplied with this erstwhile luxury good.

Most of the world's several thousand tons of indigo produced every year is synthetic. But a few remaining villages in India preserve the art of making natural indigo, which is extracted from the leaves of *indigofera tinctoria*, a perennial ground-cover plant with pink or violet flowers. To make true indigo, the leaves are soaked in water and fermented using a rather unappealing solution of ashes, cow urine, beer, and yeast. The temperature and the mixture are crucial in order for the dye to be effective. Fifteen feet deep, with bubbling scum

OPPOSITE: A pile of freshly-dyed indigo cottons. ABOVE: A Bagru printer's hand stained by the natural indigo—eventually it does wash off!

at the top, the vats have the mysterious aura of a witch's brew and are kept hidden away so outsiders can't come and steal a particular dye master's secret formula.

Indigo printing in Bagru, where I learned about it, involves a mud resist paste. Each printer has his own secret recipe for his mud resist mix, and I've never been able to convince any of them to reveal theirs to me. But basically it is a thin, meticulously formulated clay or mud-and-cow-dung mixture that the printer stamps on the fabric in patterns with simpler wooden blocks; then he leaves the fabrics to dry in the sun before they are lowered into the indigo vats—gently, so the clay won't crack off. The mud literally "resists" the dye, so what's left after the mud comes off are white patterns set off by beautiful shades of indigo.

When I tried my hand at indigo dyeing, I would print the fabrics with a layer of clay that was too thick, and the clay would crack and the dye would seep through like spider veins. You have to be very gentle when stamping the mud, as it can smudge very easily. There are not many tricks in mud printing, so it lends itself to simple blocks.

I became interested in Bagru's printing because the results weren't exactly what would be expected or traditional. As with other printing techniques, I wanted to try everything. I wanted to learn the right way and also the wrong way. I would overprint the mud to the point that the printer would be unsure if the clay would stay on in the baths. (Some of these early prints are shown later in the book.) And I would dip sheets of paper into the indigo vats to see the many shades that indigo can create with multiple dips, and I saw how with each plunge, the shades grew deeper.

OPPOSITE, CLOCKWISE FROM TOP: Application of clay resist in progress; a bucket of indigo sitting on top of a wooden vat cover; more clay resist being applied.

TENDING THE MISTRESS

Dyers often talk of the impetuous nature of indigo vats. They say they are like a mistress who needs lots of tending and attention. The dyers stir them endlessly. Once the prints are stamped in the clay resist, they have to dry in the sun and be gently lowered into the vats so the clay will not crack off. But I would print them with too-heavy clay and they would crack, which I liked.

ABOVE: One of my early forays into indigo dyeing. OPPOSITE: Indigo laid out to dry in the (very hot) sun.

Batik

Around the world, from ancient Egypt to Asia to West Africa, batik textiles have been produced for at least a millennium. But the art of batik reached its height of excellence in Indonesia, especially on the island of Java. *Batik* is originally an Indonesian-Malay word meaning "to dot." But there is more to batik, of course, than dots. Like indigo, the primary method of making batik textiles involves a resist medium. In the case of batik, the more common form of resist is used, which is wax and paraffin. Wax resists can be just as temperamental as mud resists in their formulation. Beeswax can be a little too flexible, and paraffin is prone to cracking, but just the right mix of the two makes the perfect medium. And when a design calls for a little crackling, more paraffin might be added to the mix so the dye can seep through the wax.

Batik uses blocks the same way Indian block printing does. But batik blocks are made of copper. They are works of art themselves, and look beautiful hanging on the walls on

OPPOSITE, CLOCKWISE FROM TOP LEFT: An elegant copper stamp; printers at their worktables working on dampened tables so wax won't stick to the surface; beautiful designs in wax; women drawing detailed repeat motifs; a copper stamp with star lattice; using a stencil to keep the wax contained; more beautiful designs in wax. ABOVE: Hand-drawing batiks with a tulis (wax resist pen).

pegs. Batik tables are small and padded, with layers of cotton atop the padding. The top layers are kept damp with a sponge, to make sure the wax won't stick when it is applied to the thin fabric used for batik.

Once the wax is stamped onto the fabrics, they are ready for dyeing. In batik the dye is cool, so the wax won't melt, and fabrics are dipped repeatedly into darker colors as the process goes along, with each previous color preserved by a new application of the wax resist. Once all the dips are done, the wax gets scraped or boiled off; then the fabrics get softer and softer as they are washed multiple times and left to dry in the sun.

There is a rich history of pattern design and color in traditional Javanese batik, especially in Yogyakarta, where I apprenticed in a batik workshop. Over the last three centuries, batik in Indonesia has become one of the principal expressions of spiritual and cultural values. Certain colors, such as white, blue, and brown, are considered sacred, representing the principle Hindu deities Shiva, Vishnu, and Brahma, while certain patterns have been created exclusively for the royal family and are not allowed to be worn by commoners.

WAXING POETIC

Batiking is perhaps more sensual than other forms of printing because of the sweet smell and golden color of the warm wax, the hot copper stamps, and the painstaking process of stamping, dyeing, washing, and repeating. Some designs call for the use of a small bamboo copper pen that is dipped into hot wax, like a fountain pen into ink. The pen has a spout tiny enough to hand-draw intricate designs. The artisans sit patiently drawing small, repeated motifs that will resist the next round of dye. There is a lush softness to the fabrics once they are boiled to remove the wax. The printing tables are small and intimate, and there's a different language, visually; batik motifs come from the Dutch, the Chinese, and the royal courts of Solo, a town in central Java also known as Surakarta.

OPPOSITE, CLOCKWISE FROM TOP LEFT: Ladies hand-drawing with a tulis (wax pen) on cloths draped over sawhorses, so they can be easily maneuvered for working on small sections at a time; stamp of Garuda, a mythical Hindu bird; more ladies drawing; stamped image of Javanese shadow puppet character Rama; an array of intricate copper stamps.

Ikat

The process of weaving an ikat starts long before thread hits the loom—it starts in a cocoon. Thai silk comes from silkworms that feed on the leaves of mulberry bushes. They spin their cocoons with a single thread that is 500 to 1,500 meters long. Local lore says it was the empress Si Ling Chi of China who discovered silk when she was sitting under a mulberry tree and a cocoon fell from the tree into her teacup. Extracting it from her tea, she discovered the fine, luminous thread as it unraveled. The Chinese guarded— unto death!—the secret of silk for millennia, but eventually it spread throughout Southeast Asia after a Chinese princess married an Indian prince and smuggled some silkworms out of China in her headdress.

The thread of these mulberry-eating caterpillars has a layer of protein and a triangular-shaped fiber, which give it a lustrous and smooth sheen. Since they are microthin, single threads are combined to make a thicker, more practical

OPPOSITE, CLOCKWISE FROM TOP LEFT: A weaver passes the shuttle through the warp to create the weft; looms in open air under a house; spools of pre-tied and -dyed thread ready to go onto a shuttle; weaving is a family affair—children in their family's household workshop. ABOVE: Threading the warp through the reed.

My friend and local agent, Op, would negotiate in the polite but tough Thai fashion, and work slowly and methodically to bring dealers to a reasonable deal; it helped our cause that she is almost six feet tall.

COLORS OF THAILAND

The old Thai silks are soft, rich, and deeply colored. Sarongs worn by the maids in the country are so beautiful. At the weekend market, I found acres and acres of stalls where you can buy puppies, antiques, and new jeans. There were old textiles from all over Vietnam, China, and Burma, and sometimes some from India. I am not a weaver, but I appreciate the skill and mind of weavers. They are usually farmers, and they spend their off-season weaving. I wonder if farming is somehow complementary to weaving, since they seem so exceptionally skilled with their hands at the looms.

filament. Thai raw silk has a slightly bumpy, knotty character that makes it perfect for hand-weaving and lends a rich and original quality to ikat textiles. Machine-made silk is usually made with polyester. It's smoother and lacks visible flaws and the iridescence of the real thing.

Ikat is an Indonesian word for what the Thais call *mudmee*; *mud* means "tying," and *mee* refers to the silk thread. Ikat fabric was traditionally reserved for robes used at weddings, temple ceremonies, spirit-appeasing rituals, and important social occasions. The lavish expense and expertise invested in this art resulted in spectacular quality and highly refined levels of design. Now, both men and women wear ikats as sarongs.

Before the women (who are the best Thai weavers) sit down at their looms, the threads are bundled together in small bunches and tied with waterproof bindings—usually plastic—and then dipped in dyes, which allow for two colors on each thread. The threads are then unbundled and aligned on the looms in precise patterns. Depending on which way the threads are laid out, you get a "warp" or a "weft" ikat. The warp threads are the ones tied and held in tension on the loom, and the weft threads are the ones woven under and over the warp.

Watching Thai ladies at their looms, which clack back and forth and up and down, is hypnotic. They might spend an entire week just loading the warp threads onto the loom, and then they use pedals to control the warp's up-and-down movement as they create the patterns for a warp ikat. A weft ikat is yet more complicated and involves greater expertise, because the women create the design as they go, hand-weaving the weft threads in and out of the warp, and they are able to anticipate the final look without the aid of a pattern. Using these hand looms, the weavers can produce about a yard of fabric per day.

OPPOSITE, CLOCKWISE FROM TOP LEFT: Cotton thread, pre-tied and waiting to be dyed; passing the warp to make the weft; a weaver concentrates on lifting and lowering treadles to create the pattern, counting the number of passes through the warp; tie-dye ikat on the loom; detail of an ikat in progress.

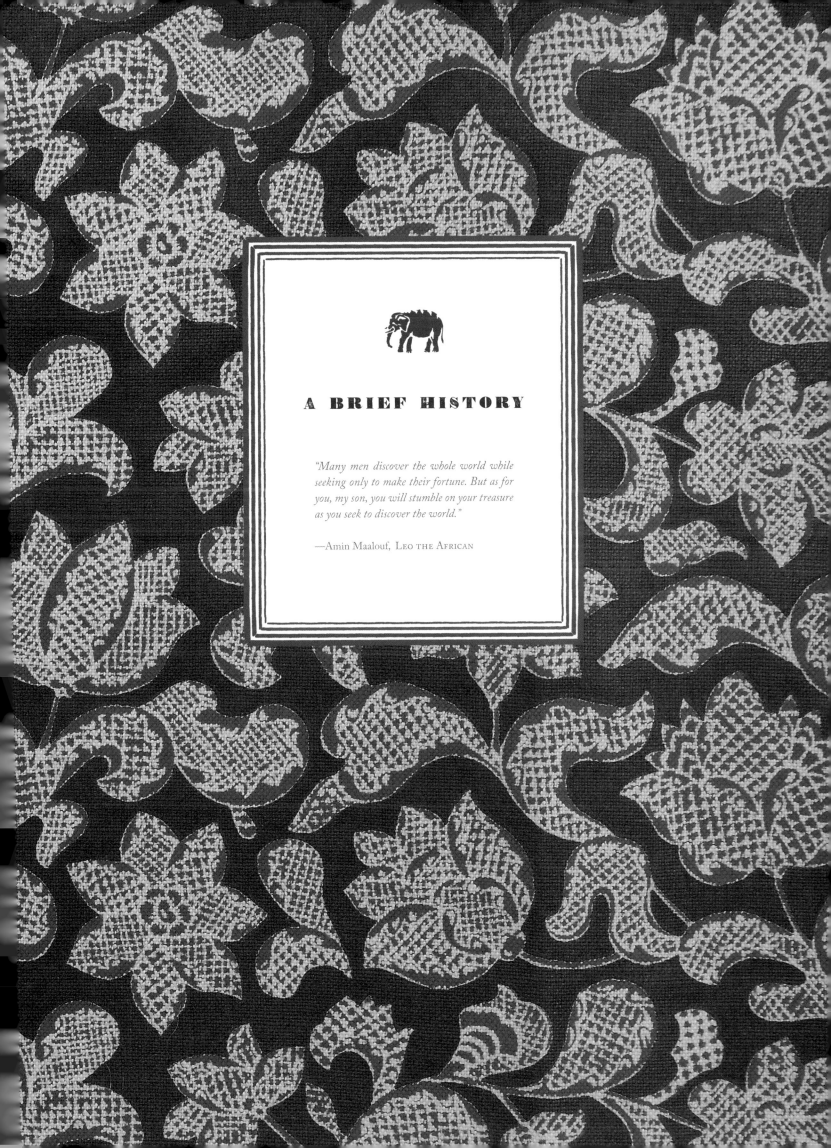

A BRIEF HISTORY

"Many men discover the whole world while seeking only to make their fortune. But as for you, my son, you will stumble on your treasure as you seek to discover the world."

—Amin Maalouf, LEO THE AFRICAN

Buffalo to Lancaster

Buffalo, New York, where I grew up, might be about as far from the spice and lore of India or Southeast Asia as one could get. My parents were a groovy married couple in the swinging '70s, going out to parties and discos—my mom in furs and cocktail dresses, my father the dandy in his sharp suits (his father had a men's shop). My mother, Mary Loy Robshaw, would say I swiped my artistic bent from her; she grew up in New York City and studied art at Duchesne (now Sacred Heart) on the Upper East Side, where she used to knock off Picassos left and right and drag my father around the museums. Her ambition was to be an interior decorator, but her parents put the brakes on, thinking that was an inappropriate sort of job. So she became a grade-school teacher and married my father in 1961, and later stayed home with my two brothers, my sister, and me. My father, John Paul Robshaw, is a self-made man who worked at a car plant to put himself through law school at Holy Cross in Worcester, Massachusetts.

Betwixt and between Buffalo's football games and bitter blizzards and country club mixers, I went to Nichols School, a liberal private high school that fostered free spirits and had some intriguing faculty: my English teacher was a former agent in the Austrian Secret

OPPOSITE: Family picture circa 1975, John flanked by brothers Chris (left) and Mark (right), in front of parents John Paul and Mary Loy. ABOVE: passport photo, age 32.

Service; he used to harangue us in front of a wall-size world map, and if we weren't paying attention he would give us the finger. In Painting we worked quietly, so as not to wake the teacher, who was inevitably asleep on the sofa.

I took my first art classes at Nichols, in skylit studios that were set apart from the main campus. I realized right away I had an addiction to art. My early paintings were a bit "confused," maybe because I was dyslexic, but I dove into photography like a crazed chemist in the darkroom, learning all the tricks of possibility and randomness in developing, and the teacher encouraged experimentation. That's when I began making what I call my early Man Ray photograms, balancing space and light with objects, and packing in the mystery. My friends included a fast crowd of studious punk rockers who introduced me to dance clubs in the decrepit husk of downtown Buffalo. And when I was sixteen, I somehow convinced my parents to let me tour Europe in a VW van with some Germans I met on a family trip to the Deep South. Once I had seen the world, I knew I had to leave Buffalo.

After graduating from high school, I entered Franklin & Marshall College in Lancaster, Pennsylvania, where I spent hours printmaking, bronze casting, life drawing, etching, and painting and jogging with my poetry teacher while we debated the meaning of everything. Shakespeare and poetry were all in the mix, so one medium influenced the others and I never settled on one thing. I couldn't see settling for one when I could mix them together and learn from them all. The great professors I had imposed very few restrictions, and the studios were open at all hours. I spent a lot of time experimenting, creating, screwing up, and discovering across mediums.

My philosophy both in art and in life was to try everything, plunge into my work with tons of energy and openness to whatever might happen, and let my aesthetic unfold along the way using any material, in any space, with anyone. One of the most liberating things I discovered during that time was the reversal of printmaking. Depending

Taking a break on a Pratt studio paint-encrusted floor.

on the technique, I could work backward, upside down. Being dyslexic, I turned everything around anyway and was always coming up with eclectic spaces and shapes.

Early on in my art education, starting in high school and college, I became preoccupied with the layers between the mark making and the outcome. I was drawn to the way printmaking let me float around an idea with my hands, and to the way incorporating different processes would slow down my hands and my head. I was delighted to discover that there is no one way to create an image—there are many ways and many routes. Nothing is set. Nothing is right. I still enjoy that today. Where in figure drawing, it really had to look like the damn figure or no one knew what you were drawing, if you didn't start from a form and didn't have to show a specific form in a certain way, magic could happen. I have always preferred this sense of charm and mystery; life grabs hold of the work that way.

Rome

Junior year in Rome in 1986 was the best year—until the money ran out. Riding around on my beat-up old Vespa in the mod suits I'd held on to since high school, I'd stop at traffic lights and smile at pretty Italian girls, statuesque in their high heels while I wobbled around on my motorbike and fell over. My lasting impressions from that year are the colors of Rome, and how decaying, falling apart, dirty, and open to discovery the city was. I had plenty of time to mull it all over, spending all afternoon out scrambling around ruins, drawing them, and sitting on them to read. I was very attracted to Rome and its decay—all these years spent falling apart and no one bothering to pick it up, and life happening right over it. One of my friends had an apartment with a fourteenth-century wall in it that he slept next to; outside his window, in the gardens, were statues with their heads lopped off.

I was at EUR (Esposizione Universale di Roma), in a fascist neighborhood on the outskirts of town. My program,

Hail Caesar! at one of Rome's many fountains.

organized by Temple University's Tyler School of Art, gave me classes in studio art history, baroque art, Greek art, Italian art, and Italian language. I zeroed in on etching and printmaking. But outside of class, I spent afternoons stealing away to local bars and long lunches with red wine, talking about art with friends, although not with the Italian fellows, who were more interested in us as a means of picking up the American girls in our school. I wandered around museums, and sat by the river with all types strolling by—heroin addicts and businessmen and lost tourists.

I took day trips to Pompeii and Herculaneum, running my hands over the marble statues when the guards weren't looking, as one of my art professors instructed me to do. He said, "In life, sometimes you must touch things when no one is looking." At night, my gang danced at clubs into the wee hours before heading home, which was ten kilometers from Rome's center, and on the way I would circle the Colosseum on my old Vespa three times for good luck.

China

During my senior year at Franklin & Marshall, I applied for a grant to study Chinese block printing at the Zhejiang Academy of Fine Arts in Hangzhou, China, the capitol of Zhejiang province. The school was founded in 1928, when China was war-torn and encouraging fine Chinese art education as a replacement for religion. The campus was full of Chinese art students who were just starting to mingle with foreigners. I felt a sense of intrigue, as I could not quite figure out what was going on culturally, but I knew there was tension in the air. We worked in old classrooms, and teachers told me about reeducation and lost years. . . . It all added to a sense of loss that was hard to fathom as a young student from America.

I plunged into the sea of bicycles on my own bicycle, and sporting a Mao suit just for fun; most of the Chinese were

Tiananmen Square.

still wearing them. I took the worthwhile risk of smuggling Chinese art students from the school out to fancy dinners (which then amounted to dinner at a Western hotel). China was barely opening up, and there weren't many foreigners around, so we were watched, for sure.

At art school, I learned the slow, painstaking process of carving printing blocks by hand, mixing the colors, and hand-painting the blocks for printing. I admired the soft watercolors on the rice paper, and the drawn-out process of carving the blocks. It all tried my patience, but it made the arrival at making my mark—getting block to paper—all the more appealing.

Block printing meant carving the reverse of what I had in mind, negative and positive. With dyslexia, it's always been a bit fuzzy for me, which I like, and I've always taken it as a consolation that I will come up with surprising patterns, thanks to being upside down and turned around. My interest in block printing was not premeditated—the life, the process, came barging in because I didn't fight the chance for errors and happenstance and the variety of mediums it offers.

During my studies that year, a pro-democracy movement was gaining momentum and led to demonstrations at Tiananmen Square. It all came to a swift end on June 4, 1989, when the government declared martial law in Beijing and killed hundreds of protesters. But some of the young, rebellious students involved in the movement were from my art school, the premier art school in China, and they were responsible for the goddess of democracy statue that made a dramatic—and abrupt—appearance at Tiananmen Square during the protests. It was designed and produced quickly out of foam and papier-mâché over metal armature, and installed on May 29. They purposely created it on a grand scale so it would not be easily dismantled; it would have to be destroyed or left there. The Ministry of State Security threatened to revoke the licenses of the truck drivers who assisted in transporting the six crates carrying pieces of the statue. *Lady Democracy* lasted only five

TOP: Under Mao's gaze at Tiananmen Gate to the Forbidden City. BOTTOM: Learning Tai Chi at West Lake in Hanghzou, Zhejiang, China.

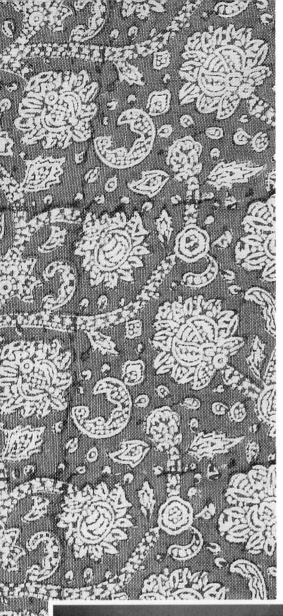

days before the People's Liberation Army destroyed it during the attack on Tiananmen Square.

I caught wind that the students were going to Beijing, to the square. Being a foreigner and not really speaking Chinese, I didn't totally understand what was going on. But we all went to see the statue and drink beer. Everyone was asking me about democracy. But what idea did I have? At that time to me, democracy meant: you do what you want! It was so foreign to me that these people could not do what they wanted—we were art students! It took time for the reality to sink in. Eventually, the soldiers ushered all the foreigners out. I flew to Hong Kong, then back to New York, and watched from afar as the movement fell to pieces, wondering how the openness and curiosity of the Chinese students would survive in such a brutal society.

New York

Back in New York and in need of work, I wove my way through the art world. A stint as a floater at Sotheby's, the New York/London/Paris auction house, afforded me access to all kinds of art, as well as the chance (between my low-level tasks) to peruse the catalogs, wear a jacket, and wander around the rare-coin department.

When the Gagosian Gallery landed on the Upper East Side, I got a job there packing and unpacking incredible pieces of blue-chip art from the likes of Ellsworth Kelly, Cy Twombly, Brice Marden, and Saatchi & Saatchi's revolving sales of '90s artists. . . . It was a heady time, with prices skyrocketing as art continually changed hands like parcels of real estate being flipped. But when I asked for a meager raise so I could continue to pay the rent on my Brooklyn hovel, I was turned down. So I left.

I ditched my suit jackets and headed for the grittier world of designer art, to the studio of Julian Schnabel, the wild child

Early painting studio in an old, abandoned squash court on William Street, New York.

of the 1980s art world, to work as one of his many assistants. He had a great setup, between his Chelsea studio and his estate (formerly Warhol's) in Montauk, Long Island. Against a backdrop of blaring opera, his cadre of assistants would lurch back and forth across the studio with heavy twenty-by-twenty-foot canvases so Mr. Schnabel could see them in different combinations. In the summer season, we would strap canvases to the walls of the open-air studio so Schnabel could throw his paint-soaked rags at them, or drench them with gallons of hurling resin as they lay flat. He was an excellent salesman, and it was fun to watch him work his magic. Occasionally, like a diva, he would emerge from his bedroom in the Chelsea studio and descend the two-story staircase wearing his bathrobe to make a sale to a dazzled collector.

The buying and selling of art in this rarefied world of galleries and art-world stars ultimately left me bereft and craving a return to a real creative process. I had been scraping by with bartending gigs, driving an art truck, working as a deckhand on a tugboat, and showing my work in group shows, but not getting anywhere. All the while, I was also studying at the Pratt Institute in New York City, working toward an MFA in painting. When I got there, I had the time to create using all the various mediums that had been left aside during my gallery days. I immersed myself almost at random in the gamut of disciplines, starting with industrial design and printmaking, then moving on to textiles, which eventually led me back to block printing.

I jumped at the chance to go to India when a professor connected me to a fashion-house supplier that needed a courier to deliver beads and dress patterns to Bombay. Once the errand was done, I had extra time to wander around and explore the world of Indian textiles, and to discover how printed fabrics were an integral part of people's lives there. Their fathers and grandfathers and great-grandfathers were block printers. It was a job, but it was also an art and a heritage. The cloth had so much life—so many people had handled it, added to it,

Early ink-washed paintings.

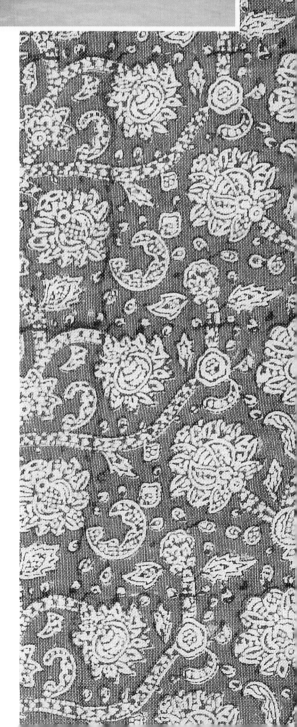

and passed it on. Each piece had its own story, which made it meaningful and useful. It was art that actually did something! I wanted to make art like that, too—art for which the process itself is the story.

Back in Brooklyn, jet-lagged and, I am sure, harboring a few new and exciting parasites, I stumbled on some cheap bolts of heavy cotton denim in a Williamsburg warehouse, and I bought the whole lot. This would make for my first big breakthrough in creating art using fabric. I tried painting on it but didn't like the results, which were too heavy and clumsy. The denim had its own beauty, and the paint interfered as an unnecessary layer. So I hauled it all up to the roof of my building and, Jackson Pollock–style, started throwing bleach across the fabric. I loved how it began to look like photographs or photograms, so I started to call the paintings "blueprints diagrams stories." The denim prints reminded me of plans for a prison escape, so I named them after a facility in upstate New York where a friend was serving time.

For another experiment, I borrowed my fashion-designer studio mate's sewing machine and made collage "paintings" out of various scraps, using the fabric as the medium by sewing patches onto canvases. I simply ran the machine wild to imitate dollops of paint. Women artists at the time were tackling feminist issues with smaller-scale artworks, and making comments on gender and "women's work." And here I sat, squarely behind my sewing machine as an aside to this movement, very taken with how interesting, vital, and dynamic the fabrics themselves were, and soon I forgot where I had started from. My color paths ran this way and that, like Pollock's paint drips, only mine were made of thick bunches of thread. I was adding colors but not hiding how the fabric was made. I loved how there were no secrets, nothing hidden—the colors only added to and enhanced the obvious.

At the same time, I was studying at Pratt. I began working for a famous video artist from Santiago, Juan Downey,

TOP: Bleach-on-denim paintings, Brooklyn apartment rooftop. BOTTOM: In Pratt studio.

executing large trace drawings for him that started with concentric circles made with a pin and a piece of string with a pencil attached—an old-school architectural trick. They turned into huge, lovely, spare paper drawings with repeated pencil-line waves going in and out of each other. Juan would give me a bottle of wine when I worked at night, which didn't help when I was trying not to mess up the rhythm of the circles. I was also his driver. I had a derelict Honda, as I was living in the hood near Pratt; it had two broken, taped-up windows, and someone stole the battery out of it one night. Juan would sit in the passenger side, and we would prowl around the Queens waterways, shooting long shots slowly from the highway. He would talk the whole time. I never knew where he would come from or where he would go with his ideas. He was very calm and interesting. His free spirit and freewheeling approach to life sparked a similar attitude in me, and I always think of him as having shaped me in some way as an artist.

Juan Downey takes aim, horsing around with friends in his loft on White Street, New York.

JUAN DOWNEY

Juan Downey was a pioneering video artist originally from Santiago, Chile, where he was born in 1940. He studied architecture in Chile and engraving in Paris, and then came to New York in 1965 to study at Pratt. He started making films with a tiny Sony Portapak video camera and traveled all over the Amazon basin making films including *Trans Americas*, *The Thinking Eye*, and *The Looking Glass*. His films were a mix between personal reflection and documentary, addressing issues of South American identity, Western attitudes, economics, and the multimedia world. He won grants from the Rockefeller and Guggenheim Foundations, as well as numerous awards, and his art was exhibited widely, including in installations at the Whitney Museum, the International Center of Photography, and the MoMA in New York, at the San Francisco Museum of Modern Art, and all over South America. He died of cancer at the age of fifty-three.

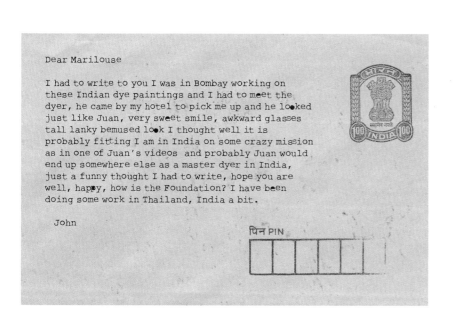

Dear Marilouse

I had to write to you I was in Bombay working on these Indian dye paintings and I had to meet the dyer, he came by my hotel to pick me up and he looked just like Juan, very sweet smile, awkward glasses tall lanky bemused look I thought well it is probably fitting I am in India on some crazy mission as in one of Juan's videos and probably Juan would end up somewhere else as a master dyer in India, just a funny thought I had to write, hope you are well, happy, how is the Foundation? I have been doing some work in Thailand, India a bit.

  John

पिन PIN

THE NATIONAL INSTITUTE OF DESIGN

Inspired by Bauhaus and Ulm in Germany, NID was set up in 1961 by the Indian Department of Industry to pioneer industrial-design education in India. The government invited Charles and Ray Eames to initiate a design program for fledgling new technology industries in India, to help them become established. Today it offers degree programs in everything from textile and interior design to transportation and architecture, as well as film and game design. Thanks to the influential presence of NID, Ahmedabad is renowned for its architectural wonders, including Louis Kahn's Indian Institute of Management, and many significant buildings by Le Corbusier that showcase his ability to infuse Indian style with his own. The city has also produced its own geniuses, including Gautam Sarabhai, who, with a design by Buckminster Fuller, built the twelve-meter-wide geodesic dome on the Calico Museum in 1962. Unfortunately, the dome collapsed in a 2001 earthquake, but it was regarded as an icon of its era.

Mumbai

My courier gigs to India took me through Paris (to pick up sequins and beads from the high-end embroidery supplier) and then to Mumbai, which was a hundred degrees and dusty. I rode around in one of those funny black-and-yellow midget circus taxis, dodging people coming from all directions in all forms of transportation—motorbikes, rickshaws, horses. I had my old Nikon strapped around my neck, and I snapped away; the dust made for great black-and-white shots. In every direction, my frames were filled with people; it seemed I could not take an uninteresting shot. The cab darted in and out of traffic, honking like it was the end of the world, but my driver smiled placidly, as if he were just out for a Sunday drive.

When I got the chance, I headed down to Goa, where I met a carnival of faltering, wasting-away hippies—elegant in their own way—selling whatever they could find, make, or steal, arranged neatly on a towel, like a beach rummage sale. They had long blond dreadlocks, heavy strands of beads and jewelry all over themselves—the world's most stylish homeless people gathered in one place.

Ahmedabad

I made my way to Ahmedabad, where I met a group of young Indian women coming out of the Calico textile museum. The late-June heat made things feel like the inside of a tandoori oven. The restaurants and shops covered their windows to keep their interiors cool, and everyone was moving rather slowly.

When these girls saw me loitering in the museum courtyard, they asked me what I could possibly be doing in Gujarat in the summer. I must have been the only tourist around. I explained how I was there to learn about block printing and Indian textiles in general, and they enthusiastically told me I had to come over to NID, the National Institute of Design, where they were all students. They said it was the best school in India for textiles. They agreed to take me there, but not for nothing. Gujarat was a dry state, but as a foreigner, I could get a license to buy liquor. "Whiskey," they said. "Get us enough to have a party." I thought, "Fair enough," and we piled into rickshaws and headed off to NID.

Thus I found myself back in school, though informally, since I was really just hanging out, sitting in classes and finding printers to work with. NID was a cool school with a '60s vibe, very mellow and eccentric. People were weaving here and there in the sprawling gardens, and huge monkeys hanging around, all in the shadows of impressive buildings by Le Corbusier, as well as the incredible Calico Museum.

The Calico houses the most impressive collection of textiles in India, with amazing variety and historical span, but an unfortunate display. The glass cases were covered in dust, and guides walked us from room to room, turning lights on and off. Once, when I went with a group of students on a tour, a crazy-old-lady guide walked us around, pointing to the grimy cases. And after viewing each antique wonder, she would say Indians "can't do this sort of work today." I could tell my fellow students, Indians all, wanted to take her out and stone her! They were studying the same techniques and knew artisans could—and did—still make these textiles.

On my thirtieth birthday, the girls I had met outside the Calico took me to the Palitana Temples, just outside Ahmedabad, in Gujarat. One of the girls was a Jain, and this was one of their main holy sites. I climbed barefoot—no shoes allowed—up the 3,800 marble steps to the awesome cluster of temples at the top that took nine hundred years to build. Hundreds more mini-temples shone out between the crags of the mountain on the way up. The monks alongside me were old and young, climbing silently in meditation, smiling even in the devastating heat. At the top, I took photographs and wandered in and out of the temples, tracing marble carvings

Friends from NID: Sona, Madhu (in the hat), John, and Ambika.

that were so fine as to seem like liquid. "This is the start of my new life," I thought, because of my birthday. And I asked for forgiveness and a string of good luck that making merit on your birthday should bring.

A few weeks into my life at NID, I heard about a local printer who lived and worked down by the river. This printer and his wife used vegetable dyes—as opposed to synthetics—and printed outside, shaded from the scorching sun only by makeshift jute awnings, which also kept the dyes from drying out. I went to meet him and made a deal that would allow me to come and print on his tables, and he would dye the fabrics in exchange for a small fee.

I can still remember the feeling of freedom I experienced when I picked up different blocks and collaged them together in all different colors, mixing them up and creating new ideas. It became addictive. I would spend all day there, forgetting about the heat, taking breaks for bottles of Thums Up cola, a local Coke knockoff, and actually better and sweeter. Mobs of amused Indians came to watch me print; word got out about this funny fellow making mistakes and misprinting, creating seemingly random designs. I learned to print with people watching, and decided not to care but to forge ahead with my experiments. I learned about Indian curiosity in all things. The printers would hover around me, amused and intrigued (or so I would like to believe).

The work I was doing there felt more like art, like paintings, than utilitarian textiles. I didn't have any commercial aspirations, yet I produced vast quantities of fabrics, working with deep, natural-colored dyes on simple homespun cloth called khadi. The dyes bled into one another, and my handiworks came out rough and intensely colored. They were somewhere between art and textiles. I wasn't sure what I was making. Large paintings? Should I mount them on wooden stretchers to show? Or was I printing yardage to hang, drape, fold—something people could live with and use, wash and hang to dry?

TOP: One of my earliest printers and his family. BOTTOM: My bemused printer watches as I overlap stamps in my unconventional way.

Either way, what I focused on was how these "paintings" could tell stories, and narrate times and places in India—its gardens, lanterns, night scenes, staircases, and hanging vines leading up and over architecture. I was trying to get it all in—the Palitana temples, the monks and mendicants, their prayers, the rush of cars moving headlong over bumpy roads. There was so much to say. I would print for hours and then start in with new colors and print new blocks on top of older ones. I would add too much dye, misalign the stamp. I became entranced by it all.

I wanted my finished pieces to reveal the process of how they were made. I wanted to see the steps behind me and show people the incredible process. They were art, they were textiles. My mind was as full, confused, and agitated as those early pieces. I was losing weight, worn down by sun and heat and hikes back and forth to the river, but felt amazed.

But I was making what I had to make, step by step. I stirred the khadi in the hot cauldron, and the dyer made up the dyes and set the trays. After we printed, we washed off excess dye from the blocks and left them to dry in the sun. The colors developed on the fabrics like photograms as they lay on the ground. Some of my earliest experiments in block printing received the high honor of having goats walk all over them while they dried, to the amusement of my fellow printers. This was no high art—it could be walked on; it could be boiled in a cauldron. The colors were rich, deep stains of earthy vegetable dyes, not a wide-ranging spectrum. But I didn't need much more; I had found my passion, and I was hooked.

Bangkok

I returned to New York for about a year following my time at NID and lived off of selling my one-of-a-kind block prints to various decorators and friends. Once I had dispensed with my full collection, I headed off again, this time to Thailand. I wanted to explore traditional ikat weaving and see the process

TOP: Some original designs dry in the sun (and a goat ready to pounce!). BOTTOM: Monkeying around with colors.

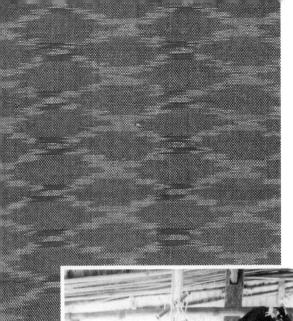

firsthand. Bangkok was home to the legendary Jim Thompson, who discovered the craft of Thai ikats and was one of my early influences. I traveled first to Isaan in the northeast, near the Laos border, to see the exquisite, labor-intensive work being done there.

I would take a train to Nong Khai, and taxis from there to small villages in the area, all rich with weavers, who, as farmers, when they weren't out harvesting, wove diligently below their solid teak houses mounted on stilts. I could hear the *click-clack* of the looms as soon as I walked up to the villages. Weaving's reverse engineering was always magic to me because of my dyslexia. The trick was to envision the end results first, then work backward to achieve it: setting up the loom, tying and dyeing the yarns, plotting out the patterns and how to weave them. It is a process that demands a patience I do not have! I was awed by the variety of the designs, which every time reflected the hand and style of their weavers, experts who relied on farming to live and on weaving to enjoy life.

On ikats I commissioned when I began to sell textiles, I didn't alter the designs or printing methods as much as I did with block prints or batiks, since I never had never gotten my own hands into the weaving process. I let the colors and natural dyes speak, and respected the simple geometric designs the weavers chose.

When I wasn't visiting the ikat weavers, I took several trips to Laos and Cambodia to witness for myself their printing techniques, which I had previously only read about. I also did a little work for a department store in Bangkok, called Wave. Paul Nisky, the American boss, hired me after I showed him a pile of batiks I had just made in Java. I had plans with Paul to develop a product for the store that never got off the ground because of the great economic crash in Asia. But I stayed on, mostly doing promotional work for the store and taking long lunches with Paul. My best accomplishment was persuading him to get out to Krabi for beach weekends and long nights of disco dancing. After eight months of that, I realized I had to get back to New York and really do something. Bangkok life was too easy and fun; I hankered for the edge of New York.

An ikat weaver in Isaan.

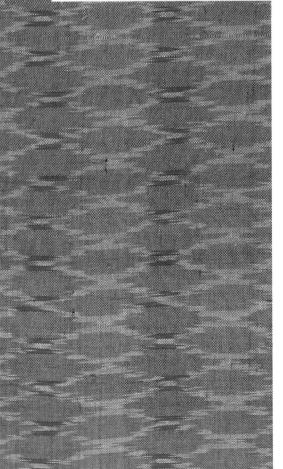

Jim Thompson with his pet bird "Cockatoo" in front of a house near the Klong River.

JIM THOMPSON

Rightly deserving his revered place in the textile world, Jim Thompson is one of my own early inspirations. He was born in 1906 in Delaware, attended Princeton, and then studied architecture at the University of Pennsylvania. Eventually he joined the Delaware National Guard and ended up serving in the Office of Strategic Services during World War II. On active duty, he parachuted into Thailand, where he remained after the war and embarked on a career as a designer and Thai silk producer, eventually forming the Thai Silk Company. Thompson's business really got off the ground when the costume designer Irene Sharaff used his designs for the original musical version (and later the film) of *The King and I*. His company nourished, promoted, and revived Thailand's dying textiles industry and lifted thousands of the country's poorest people out of poverty by relying—for the bulk of its production—on women artisans who made textiles in their homes, thus allowing them to become breadwinners. Thompson also worked to preserve Thailand's heritage, collecting Buddhist sculpture and paintings, Benjarong pottery, and blue and white ceramics. He showcased them in old Thai houses he connected together to create an elegant mansion on the Klong River, where he entertained visitors who came from all over the world, the way a former spy might do. He disappeared in 1967 while he was out for a walk in the Malaysian highlands—a cinematic ending to such a life.

SETTING UP SHOP

"There is a tide in the affairs of men.
Which, taken at the flood, leads on to fortune;
Omitted, all the voyage of their life
Is bound in shallows and in miseries.
On such a full sea are we now afloat,
And we must take the current when it serves,
Or lose our ventures."

—William Shakespeare, Julius Caesar, Act IV,
Scene 3, Brutus

New York

A fter my year of learning and leisure in Thailand, I returned to New York, as I knew I had to leave Bangkok or I would never move forward. I hustled about town with my carpetbags full of hand-printed textiles I had made, bleedy block prints on loose hand-wovens over prints in deep, moody vegetable dyes. I started painting again, and friends started buying my canvases. They would come to my East Village studio and see these mounds of fabric on the floor and ask me what they were. I had no answer! I was still noncommittal; were they textiles or art? But they liked what they saw, and asked me for more.

Elizabeth Mayhew, whom I'd met through a friend, wrote me up in *House Beautiful*. I look back on that article as the soft "launch" of my career, because it unleashed a flood of decorators calling and coming over to my studio (and thus helping me pay off my art-school loan!). Michael Smith, Peter Marino, and other decorators were among my first clients. Mostly, I saw it as a great chance to sell the textiles and travel back to small towns in Southeast Asia, where I wanted to try new printing techniques. It was the exploring, the finding, the making that was driving me, not so much the money,

OPPOSITE: In New Delhi on a chai break with my "fixer" (someone in India who troubleshoots all-and-sundry sticky situations) named Shiva. ABOVE: My first New York showroom at 245 West 29th Street, circa 2001.

DIGGI PALACE

This hotel was built as a palace in the 1860s and is set on acres of gardens. The rooms were converted within the harem side of the structure, with its big, empty spaces and thick stone walls that keep the heat in on cool days. The place has moaning showers and marble floors, and when I arrived in 1986, the beds were made with sheets that had "1974" sewn into them. I told the hotel to stop having years embroidered on its sheets if it was going to keep them that long. Outside, the gardens are full of flowers and squawking peacocks, and great for lounging and drinking chai. A funny family has run the place as long as I can remember: there is Wilson, the good-humored concierge, and Tutu, the manager, who looks like a football player with earrings and a big smile, and Tutu's uncle Nana and aunt Jyotika, the patriarch and matriarch, who sit in the garden having tea and feeding their peacocks. They offer their doctor if someone gets sick (foreigners notoriously come down with a range of illnesses that keep him very busy). After all these years, Diggi Palace is still my home base when I'm working on a new collection in India.

except insofar as I needed it to buy my next round of plane, train, and ferry tickets.

A friend who sold suits at Calvin Klein told me that the CK designers often bought prints and patterns for garments. I got a meeting with the assistant to the assistant to the assistant to show my wares. Eventually the boss came in and was smitten with these four- and five-yard pieces I had all over the room. I was taken aback when he made me an offer on the whole set. The pivotal moment was when he asked my price per textile, per print, and I had no clue what to say. But he was kind enough to whisper the going rate in my ear, and we had a deal. I felt then and there I had stumbled into a good business opportunity, and I decided to try the other big labels: Polo Ralph Lauren, Giorgio Armani, Donna Karan.

Everyone bought some prints, but I wasn't crazy about life as a salesman with a suitcase full of prints. I didn't love negotiating with the fashion industry, and felt like I was selling my soul just to get back to India. And much of what I was selling were one-offs I had made by hand. I wasn't really benefiting the artisans in India in the long run—something I was determined to do—and they kept asking me when I would start placing orders. They pushed me, which they are very good at. And I welcomed the encouragement, because I hadn't thought of my work as a product to sell, nor was I sure how it even made sense as a product.

Key Connections

The next time I went back to India, I was staying at the Diggi Palace, my usual hotel in Jaipur, and I met Alexander Gorlizki, the British artist who makes Indian miniatures based on a six-hundred-year-old Mughal style. He happened to be traveling around India and wanting to set up shop in Jaipur to work with an Indian miniature-painting master. Alex and I got to talking and discovered we were at similar stages in our

OPPOSITE, CLOCKWISE FROM TOP LEFT: At Diggi Palace, a peacock on the garden terrace; main entrance to Diggi Palace; tea time in the garden; promo for fabric line Fall 2010, shot at a railway station in Jaipur; Jyotika, the Diggi Palace matriarch; an Alexander Gorlizki miniature he made for my Spring 2008 bedding promo; Diggi Palace gardens; a birthday gift for me from Alexander Gorlizki.

HOTEL
Nirwana
11 Jl Dr. Wahidin Pekalongan 51101

SEPT 29

HELLO ALEXANDER

SORRY I DIDN'T FAX YOU BACK SOONER BETWEEN ISLANDS BURNING
PLANES CRASHING SEARCHING FOR QUOTAS FOR FABRIC. IN BALI I
WAS A MADMAN DASHING ABOUT ON MY STUPID OLD DUTCH BIKE NOW
BECAUSE OF THE GODS I AM IN SINGAPORE SINCE MY FLIGHT TO
BANGKOK WAS "DISCONTINUED" BUT THEY PUT US AT A PLEASANT
HOTEL AND I HAVE DESTROYED THE BUFFET AND CHATTED UP SOME
NIKE-ENCASED JAPANESE GIRLS SO THERE IS SOME MORAL IN ALL
THIS.

YOUR PROPOSITION SOUNDS QUITE INTRIGUING. WE WILL HAVE TO
HAVE A BINDI/HANKERCHIEF SUMMIT. I WILL BE IN INDIA OCT
15-NOV 20??? AT DIGGI PALACE. I HAVE TO SIT DOWN AND MAP IT
OUT WITH YOU. I LIKE THE ART ANGLE/SILK ROUTE PATH BUT WANT
TO MAKE LOADS OF MONEY SELLING AMERICANS RATTAN PLACEMATS,
ART I AGREE BUT TO HOW/WHY WILL NEED SOME STRUCTURE. I WILL
SIT DOWN AND WRITE OUT MY MISSION STATEMENT TO YOU NEXT WEEK
IN THAILAND BUT AM EXCITED TO TALK TO YOU. WILL BE IN NY NOV
20TH ON...YOU CAN STAY IN MY TENEMENT HOUSING.

TAKE CARE KIND ALEX

missions, both of us bustling about, making things and trying new mediums and ideas, sharing the same bottom line: we had to make it work! We each had the drive and the ideas for expanding our respective art into a livelihood, but not so much the know-how. A friendship was born, and it was nice to have a comrade to share the trail with as we figured out the twists and turns of negotiating transcontinental production with Indian artisans, getting into New York shows, and building up our enterprises.

Getting into the trade-show world was my next hurdle, if I wanted to sell to stores and graduate from my traveling-salesman routine. I needed to make myself known to stores, and the industry shows are where buyers from all over and, to a lesser extent, decorators, come to buy merchandise. The New York show is as big as it gets, and takes place at the

Early trade show, wearing a kurta.

Jacob Javits Center, a place as garish as it is remote, in the hinterlands of Manhattan on the West Side Highway. More than thirty-five thousand visitors from eighty-five countries descend on hundreds of thousands of square feet of exhibit spaces representing hundreds of categories, from tableware and garden tools to baby clothes and home textiles.

In those early days, to me the show itself felt like a shantytown, full of small hovels with shared walls and people gossiping. All that was missing were people trading chickens and rolling dice to pass the time, as we waited for buyers to come by. Most of the vendors' booths at least had press kits and price lists. I, on the other hand, set up a souklike jumble of a tent against a back wall, near the bathrooms, with sheers blocking any view into my booth. Inside, I had heaping piles of block prints from India, batiks from Indonesia, ikats from Thailand, and silks from Cambodia, along with my own designs and fabrics I'd made myself. They hung on the walls and draped over the flap of my "tent," hiding me from passersby. Buyers had to fold back the sheers to peer in as I sat on a pile of quilts. I didn't have a price sheet. People peppered me with all kinds of questions, and I muddled through with limited answers. As I had learned from the Indians, always say yes, then figure out how to do it later.

Some of my wares didn't even make sense for buyers or decorators because of their size or shape or unpredictable color lots and their handmade quality. But I wanted textiles to be that way, to be honest, just the way I like everything to be in life. I'm all about new mediums and ideas, throwing them all in and letting people sort out what to do with them.

I got better at the trade end of things as I started to establish new clients. Charles Jacobsen, a decorator and world-traveling tastemaker from Los Angeles, was supportive of my work right away. At his invitation, I went to L.A. to hang some long sari sheers he commissioned for his (most amazing) showroom. He was one of my first clients, and, in truth, I owe him my life; I took his early support as a real vote

TOP: My wares at the 2005 International Contemporary Furniture Fair trade show.
BOTTOM: Charles Jacobsen with custom-printed sheers for his L.A. showroom.

of confidence. In effect, I tripped, tumbled, and stumbled into business, starting to work a bit with stores such as Takashimaya, Felissimo, and ABC Carpet.

I decided to rent my first showroom in August 2001, in the garment district on West Twenty-ninth Street in Manhattan, one of the cheapest blocks in New York, and around the corner from a methadone clinic and the infamous Bikini Bar. My timing may not have been perfect—it was one month before the attack on the World Trade Center downtown, and after that the economy tanked—but, having just started out, I didn't have much to lose. Within six months, I felt things pick up, maybe because people were not traveling as much and instead began to think more about their homes and spending money on them. My notion of bringing world textiles home for people proved to be a timely, if unwitting, business strategy.

Jaipur

The cutthroat nature of the textile business means I have had to guard the identities of my workshops carefully (here, the names of my amazing Indian partners have been changed for my protection). Buying agents from larger companies have been known to go so far as to follow me from my hotel and bribe my rickshaw driver to find out whom I work with. But I won't give away my sources so easily. I had to bump around these cities and villages on bad roads for ten years, half a world from home, to find the right people to work with, so, I figure, others can do the same.

An NID professor recommended my first block-printing partner to me. He told me that if I was serious about printing, I had to go to Jaipur, for its centuries-old tradition of block printing, and there I had to meet Vikram. Vikram had spent years working for one of the largest block-printing companies in India and had just set out on his own. I became one of his first clients, and since we were both just starting out, in a way

ABOVE: My first showroom in New York, on West 29th Street. OPPOSITE: CLOCKWISE FROM TOP LEFT: Silk sarongs drying at Vikram's workshop in Sanganer; taking stock of a day's block-printed heavy cotton blankets; a printer shouldering fabrics dyed and ready for printing; exterior of Vikram's workshop, walled in rush; group of printers wearing aprons made from recycled fabrics; stirring printed fabrics in cauldron of hot vegetable dye; with Vikram at the workshop at the end of a day's project.

PRINTER'S EXCUSES

In one of my first journals, I found this list of reasons Vikram gave me to explain why a certain order I'd placed was not finished. I kept the list in case Vikram used the same excuse twice. I would call him on it; then he would smile and make up a new excuse.

REASONS PRINTERS HAVE GIVEN FOR WHY SHIPMENTS OF HAND-PRINTED TEXTILES WERE DELAYED OR DAMAGED:

1. The printer was stung by a wasp.

2. Pigeons on the roof left droppings on the fabrics, discoloring them.

3. The fabric washer damaged the fabric.

4. The batches of dyes were slightly different colors.

5. The neighbor's dog walked over the textiles drying in the sun and damaged them.

6. It's a festival; all the printers are gone.

7. There's been a murder in the village, and all the roads are closed while they look for the murderer.

we learned together as we went along. Vikram was happy to have the company, and I was happy to learn all of the mind-boggling steps required in India to get fabric block-printed.

In those early days, we slammed around on miserable roads, knees bumping in his tiny Maruti, first to examine fabric for defects, next across town to pick up dyes, and then to block carvers to drop off drawings to be carved into blocks. All of these stops required lengthy explanations, some including smiles, others harangues, threats, and money changing hands. One of Vikram's *dhobis* (the people who wash the fabrics after dyeing) mistook me for a Bollywood actor, and Vikram was clever enough to use that to our advantage in order to get our orders filled faster. At each stop, he spent a lot of time explaining just what he wanted. I had to learn to let go of my specific vision and be open to interpretations. Every block carver has his own interpretation of a design, or might not; sometimes, just in the tracing or carving of a design, a detail may get lost in translation. But either way, adjustments happen, and they are part of the process and randomness of working with multiple people to make something. The many hands that touch, carry, wash, carve, and dye are going to leave their mark in subtle—and sometimes not-so-subtle—ways. On occasion, an Indian printer might listen to me, but would then just do it his way anyway.

Often I purposely used the oldest printers in the unit because their hands shake and they misregister the blocks slightly, whereas the younger printers can be like machines, lining up the blocks perfectly. I have never wanted to make my merchandise in the conventional, straightforward manner. Who would need me for that? Vikram would complain that I was ruining the printers by letting them make mistakes, even begging them to misprint and be a bit sloppy to make the printing process more visible. He felt I was negating the quality-control standards he had worked hard to set in place. I tried to explain that I liked my fabrics to reveal the hand that made them, which meant letting the process show and allowing

Madhu and Tibbs. Tibbs complained in his early days that "no other printshop owner would mix his own color."

the mistakes and the passage of time to come through in the final product. These conversations would end with my assuring Vikram that I had been a mediocre printer in a past life.

After I had been working with Vikram for some time, I reconnected with another couple, Madhu and Tibbs, whom I had met at NID when we were all students. (Madhu was one of the girls in the group who had asked me to buy them whiskey.) These two had since gotten married and started a printing unit on the roof of their apartment building. Tibbs still ran his family's pharmaceutical sales business, but on the side he was mixing dyes for the new print shop, as they couldn't afford to hire a color master.

Madhu and Tibbs are a clever and interesting couple, laughing all the time, and they have a broad knowledge of textile design, so we immediately worked well together. We were all sorting our businesses out, and I couldn't think of a more fun couple to learn with. I began working with them because we shared a lot of the same design sensibilities and we pushed each other. Vikram's expertise was in more traditional Rajasthani prints, which have a huge market in Europe, and I wanted to try something new. As I worked with Madhu and Tibbs, who had both studied fashion and focused on excellent finishing details, my business began to grow and the quality of my products improved.

While working in India is highly creative and satisfying, it can be a bit of a mystery and a nightmare to the outsider some days. There is a charm to the built-in chaos in the way things get done—or don't get done! It is the ultimate "go with the flow," "breathe in, breathe out" working environment, one that I had to get used to as a hyper American who needs to keep things moving. India taught me how to juggle. Things would falter, stall, conk out, and I would just pick up something else and move ahead with it, until that fell to pieces; then I'd jump back to the other project. . . . This is the distinctive India trait: to juggle twenty-three balls at the same time and still stay cool in the tandoori-oven heat.

Bagru

When I was working with Vikram, I experimented in Bagru, the famous indigo-printing center outside of Jaipur. I made some dipped-paper drawings by plunging pieces of handmade paper (made from fabric waste) a quarter of the way or halfway into the indigo vats and letting the dye lap up the paper like a wave on the beach, then laying them out to dry across the field in the sun, with rocks holding them down. I also tried overprinting South Indian woven-cotton plaid saris. Initially they were painfully bright, but they became soft and mysterious once I overdyed them in indigo. I used very simple geometric prints on top of the wovens. I had my blocks carved more deeply than traditional ones, to keep my prints spare and modern; indigo-printing blocks are not nearly as intricate as those used for block printing, because of the mud resist method, which calls for stamping a gentle imprint on the fabric with mud-and-cow-dung paste.

Far from Jaipur, Bagru was sleepy. Time there slowed to the pace of the stamp-stamp-stamping of blocks. Sometimes the process felt like slow motion—or no motion—with its many steps: a boy mixing the clay, then pressing it through a sieve, then taking more steps and more care than with other methods. Making the vegetable dyes took longer, too, but achieved soft, warm, dusty grays, blacks, yellows, and pinks. And the clay resist had to be stamped so gently that it, too, slowed down the whole process. Then the fabric had to be moved from table to lawn to dry—slowly, so as not to smudge the clay.

Because indigo was a much slower process than other forms of block printing, it was not as much fun for me. There were fewer variables to play with, and I had to be much more precise than I liked to be. But I have always begun with a process, then figured out what I could achieve through a particular medium. It is only then, after working in the trenches and playing with techniques, that I can come up with

A spectrum of newly dyed fabrics.

how something might fit into the larger context of my designs. I decide, almost as an afterthought, what kind of product I might be able to make with a certain fabric.

Java

Back when I was concentrating on block printing in India, I was also poring over books to learn about hand-printing traditions and methods from all over the world. Indonesian batiking was one method that drew me to Java. I didn't know anyone in Indonesia, but I knew that Yogyakarta was the main town for batik. I had seen the movie *The Year of Living Dangerously*, and I figured I could pull off the large-American-in-a-bad-batik-shirt role. So I hopped a plane to Jakarta and a train to Yogya, as the locals call it. Just as I had done in Jaipur, I hired a taxi driver to take me from studio to studio, to see whom I could print with. I eventually met Mr. Hadi and his sons, a family that was still making hand-printed batiks. Mr. Hadi was very open and understanding, and he kindly let me print my own batiks on his tables—the same kind of start I got in India.

The heat and heavy wax of batiking made this a trickier business than block printing. With block printing, I could see my progress and adjust what I was doing as I went along. With batik, I had to keep the tables damp and plan ahead, and know where I was going with it. As a result, my batiks came out simpler and more graphic than my block prints. I experimented with different fabrics— loose, hand-woven cottons that hid the full outline of blocks I overprinted; old, soft-colored batik sarongs from the market, to which I added layers. I tried my shaky hand at hand-drawn batik tulis, which involves a tool with a bamboo handle and a copper spout, like a writing pen you have to refill constantly, for drawing ever-so-delicate lines with hot wax.

OPPOSITE: Balancing act—hanging a day's sheers to dry on scaffolds.

I would often scour the markets for exciting fabrics on which to print. I found deep tobacco and indigo batik sarongs in antique shops, and old royal prints in market stalls from the Yogya and Solo Courts, which I loved for their deep, dark browns and original styles and motifs. The sales ladies were all wearing them with their traditional blouses as they presided over their upper stalls deep in the market, their wooden cabinets overflowing with these precious textiles. I would carefully page through their piles, looking for the most unique and unusual odd colorations on hand-drawn batiks. The ladies there were clever; they knew which ones were the best, and I had to bargain hard for them.

Business in Indonesia was less organized than in India, and the resources were mostly the scale of a cottage industry. I had a difficult time sourcing base fabrics from the mills, which were few. Batiking can be done only on thinner fabrics, and it was difficult to find many satisfactory options. Nevertheless, for some time, I brought back yardages of batiks from my visits and commissioned many orders of hand-printed batiks for clients in New York. For B Five Studios, we reprinted all of the batiks Aerin Lauder used to cover the walls of an entire room in her Hamptons beach house, a re-creation of a room her grandmother Estée Lauder had done in the 1960s. I used the same workshop which had printed the original batiks in Pekalongan, an old batik town in Java.

My time in Indonesia was magical. There were not many foreigners in Yogya, unlike in Bali. I remember long motorbike drives through fields and past palm trees, out to the Java Sea, where, legend has it, the sea goddess would take you down in the heavy, ominous waves if you wore green. I believed it but I loved to swim, so I made sure my bathing suit was blue. I hiked up active volcanoes and wandered in and out of the Buddhist temple of the Borobudur and the Hindu temples nearby. At night I sat in the main square, watching public puppet shows of the *Ramayana*, an ancient Sanskrit epic, and heard gamelan orchestras play their xylophones, bells, and gongs in the city palace.

A Balinese ceremony.

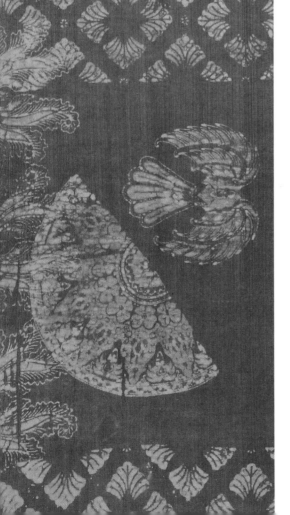

The Muslim printers I worked with took breaks five times per day to pray, which made for a very different rhythm in the workshops than in India. Throughout the day, the call to prayer would filter through the heat, and everything would come to a standstill. As in India, we printed out in covered sheds with hot coal heaters next to us, where lumps of beeswax and paraffin melted together in small skillets. All the printers had clove cigarettes dangling from their lips as they printed in the extreme humidity. (I loved those clove smokes after a spicy meal, as the ends were coated in sugar.) The pace was that of prayers, of a clove cigarette burning down slowly, of the wafting scents of beeswax. The printers would return after praying and begin again, recharged. Outside, chickens fought in the yard, while I ate *gado gado* (vegetables in a coconut peanut sauce) out of green banana leaves and listened to the distant sounds of bikes and bells.

I have vivid memories of these days in Yogya. The printers all smiled and were curious about what I was doing in their midst—this funny, large white man printing and sweating in the heat, making crazy batiks. The friendliness and openness of these people stays with me, and I remember hoping their calm nature would stick to me like wax on those lovely old copper stamps.

TOP: Fighting cocks against backdrop of batiks. BOTTOM: Copper stamps.

MARKING MY WAY

"It is a wonderful thing how the individuality of every man minutely determines his every thought and action like a penetrative dye, permeates even the most insignificant part of them so that the entire life course, the inner and outer of each one differs fundamentally from that of others."

—Arthur Schopenhauer, ESSAYS AND APHORISMS

As my wandering path of printmaking has unfolded before me, I have come to realize that textiles are what keep me tethered to the world. Each piece I make is an amulet—a textured, colored, and printed story in itself—that represents not just a place and a method, but the people, sights, sounds, and adventures I met with along the way to creating it. From printing and dyeing to hand-stitching and one-of-a-kind hand-painted pillows, the details in some of the pieces shown on these pages reveal—or in some cases skillfully obscure—the expertise, labor, and artistry involved in the process. But they all come about through a convergence of things and are not always premeditated or carefully planned out.

I keep an open mind as I approach every season, and I take trips to new as well as familiar places every several months—and always keep a ticket back to India in the mix. With every new encounter, every twist and turn of my itinerary, each new person I meet or detail that jumps out at me as I go, I am shown the way to what I should make next. I'm surprised by the many ways in which my inspiration comes: maybe I'm dodging traffic within an inch of my life in Mumbai, or navigating the roads of Kathmandu around lazy cows munching piles of marigold garlands—cast aside after religious ceremonies—or recovering from a bad case of chikungunya acquired just after the monsoons, or walking a tightrope over rice paddies to reach a Tibetan monastery (and actually falling down into the paddies), or looking at dusty, patched-together Iznik tiles in Rüstem Pasha, my favorite mosque in Istanbul.

My color ideas might come from the faded sadhus' robes at the Pushkar Full Moon Festival, or from the diagonally printed turbans I see in Jodphur's Old City, or from the remnants of block printing that seep through layers of cloth after days on the printing tables, or the caked blue hands of the indigo dyers and the wooden stick they use to turn the baths.

I can't plan designs. I rely on randomness and impatience. Things go wrong again and again, but India has taught me to keep moving, and that it will all work itself out—and if not, so be it. Life is a sloppy, chaotic patchwork that, amazingly, comes together to make a blanket one can sleep under. I try to capture that sense of adventure, confusion, touch, and breath in my textiles.

OPPOSITE: A rickshaw, newly upholstered and loaded with new prints, promotes the Spring 2011 line.

Opposite: I bought a monk's robe in Thailand, because I was interested in working with that specific shade of orange. So I brought it with me to Yogyakarta to try some batik printing. I was unsure how the dyes would react with the fabric, but the result is this print on the facing page. I shakily, nervously printed a double impression of a stamp with the wax. When dyed, the fabric did not in fact absorb the color evenly. I was happy to see that it turned out to be a good thing.

Page 116: I often bought old batiks in the markets of Solo or Yogyakarta, such as the one here, and I printed them using simple stamps, fully covered with wax, so the old design would be visible. The results are layers of interesting textures and patterns, with the original designs peering through.

Page 117: Something about this print reminds me of the Shroud of Turin. All fabrics take dye differently, and this handloom cotton shawl, with its uneven edges and texture, makes for some surprising color outcomes. I stamped this piece with light grids and then dip dyed it. The final product looks like it was unearthed in some archeological dig.

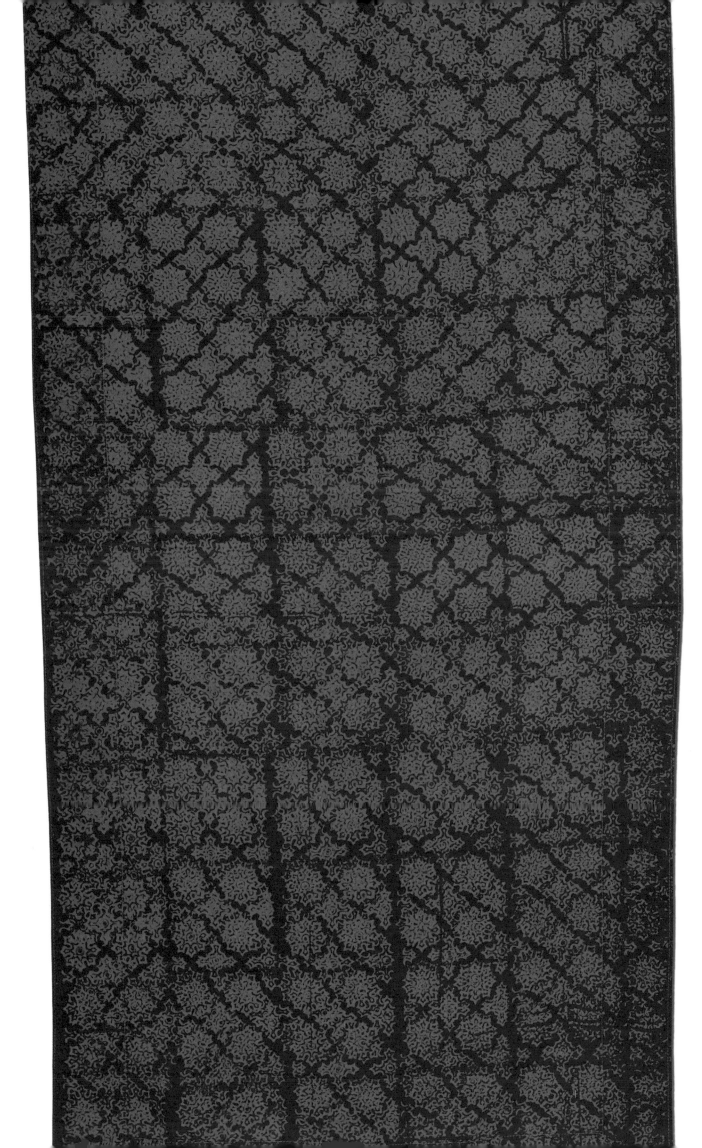

Opposite: *Khadi*, which means cloth in Hindi, were the first fabrics I liked to buy in my early days. They came in lovely soft colors and I would print with abandon and chaos, ravishing the textile. This is one of the first ones I did in Ahmedabad, where I would print with many different stamps, making up some story in my mind about Moghul gardens, trellis walls, and flowers, and telling it from an aerial view.

Page 120: This design was created using a simple lotus block, half printed with dye, and half wax stamped to create the impression of extra petals, then turned around and printed again. I dyed it in deep Solo-nut browns, the shades traditional batik makers were using for the local markets.

Page 121: A traditional batik sarong features this common batik stamp running along on the bias. Here, I popped the stamp over and over on top of itself, creating the look of a nervous dance, or a crowded bus barreling into town.

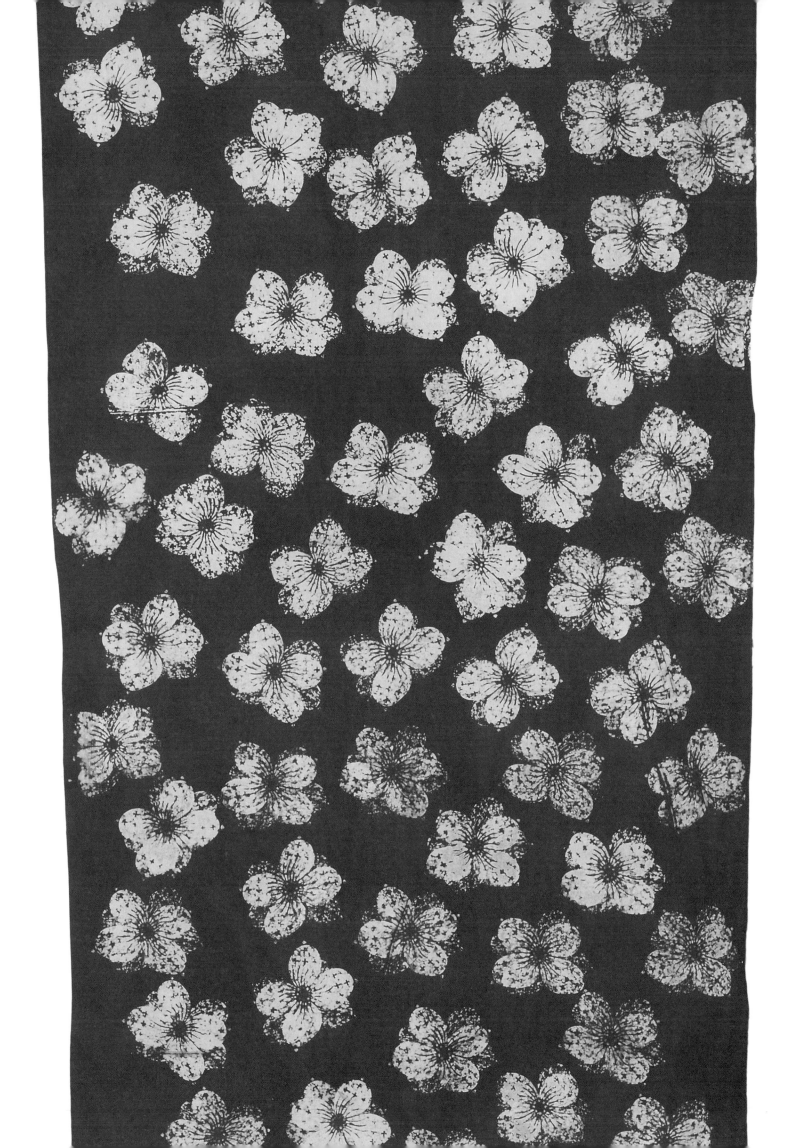

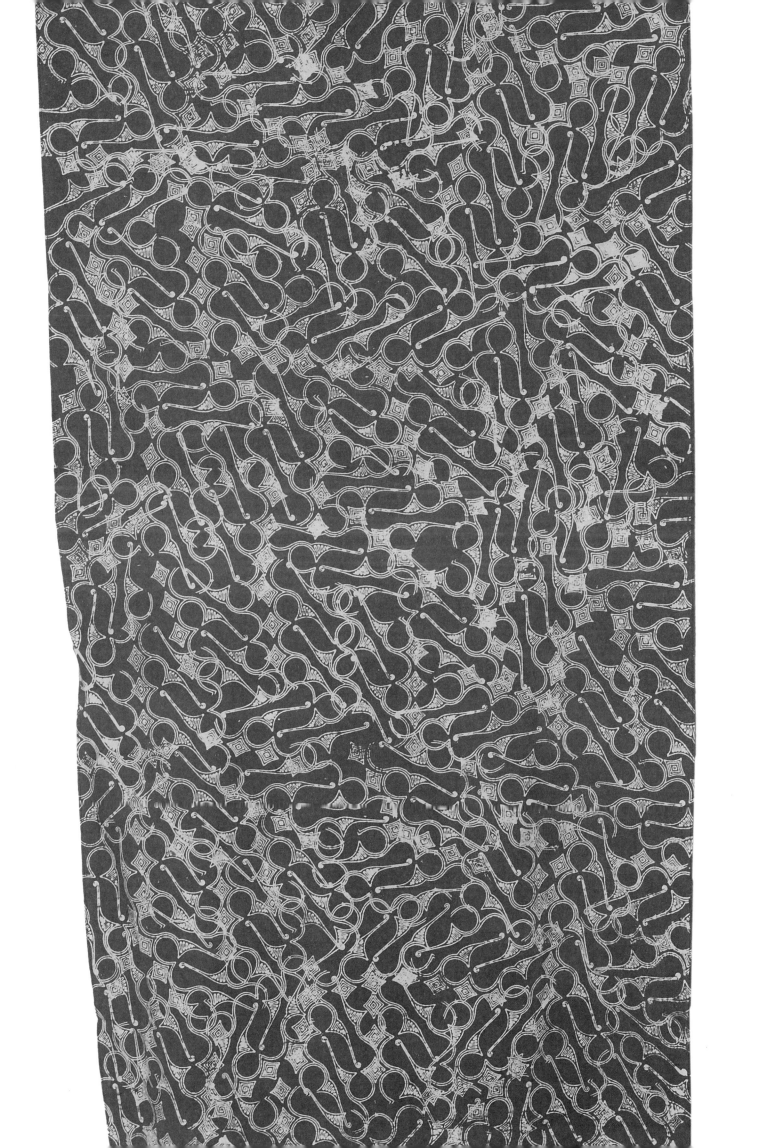

Opposite: Even though I made this print many years ago, I can still see it heavy with wax being dipped into the dyes. I had no clue what it would become, but I started marking with a block carved into a delicate grid, then printed another full block on top of that one, so now you see a window into another scene, just out of sight.

Page 124: Going a bit random with the wax on this batik, I used a traditional block that I stamped side by side but at various angles. Where less of the wax was printed, more of the negative space moves in on the perky blue.

Page 125: I used one stamp, repeated over the loosely-stretched textile to get this wavy, mis-registered grid against a background of images depicting the Hindu bird god Garuda swooping around.

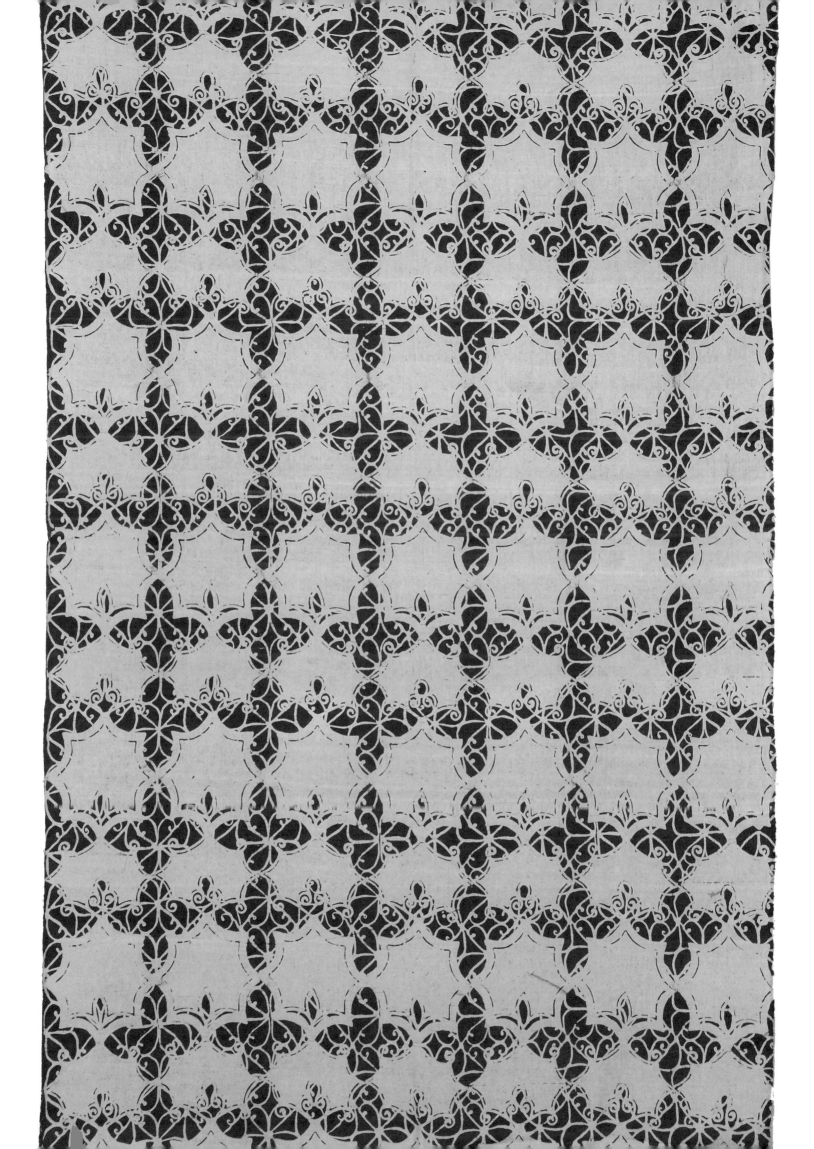

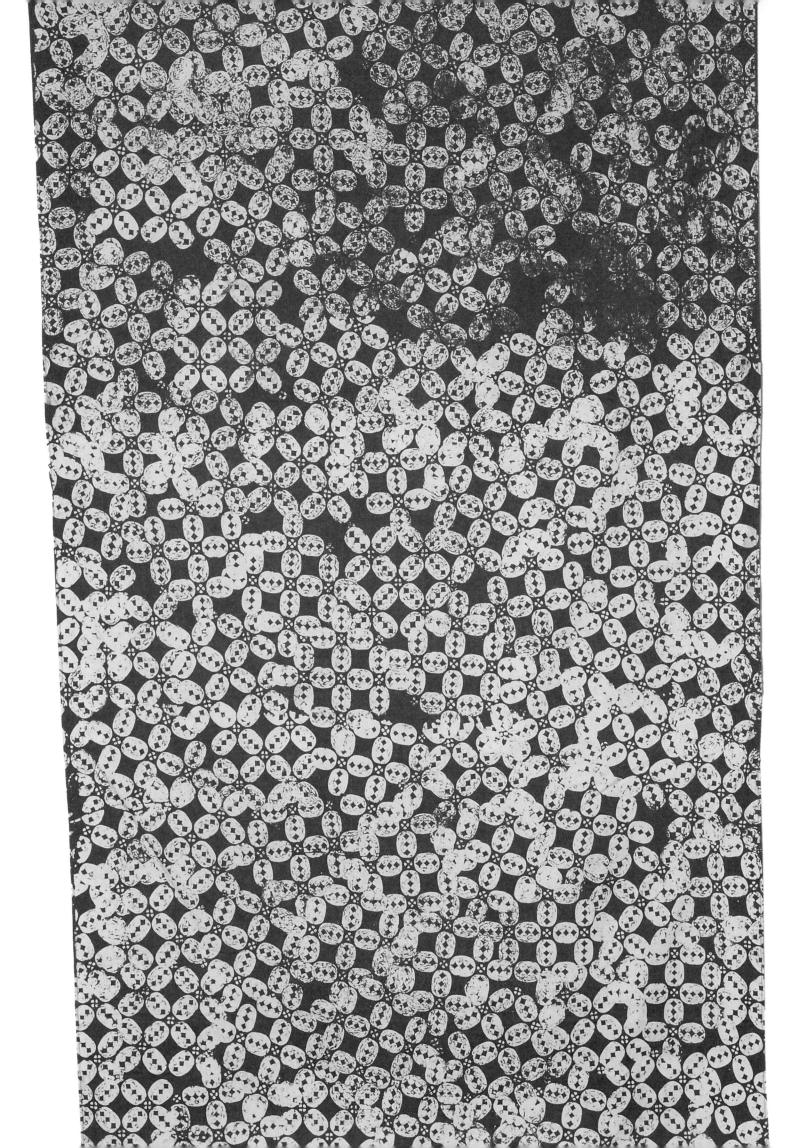

Opposite: The Solo court batiks feature this same deep chocolate dye and its rich red tinge. Here I used multiple stamps whose overlain impressions lure you down paths of flowers. It reminds me of nights I spent listening to gamelan music playing in the villages of Indonesia.

Page 128: Soft cotton took the dye only reluctantly in this print. I started with an oddly shaped circular stamp that wanted to form a circle, but I stopped it short. The result is a field of flowers springing up at a moment's notice. So much energy is contained in these layers of stamps that this print still holds my attention all these years later.

Page 129: This is one of my earliest block prints from Bagru. I printed using a trellis block, one stamp on top of another, to create mystery and dimension. Then I over dyed it in deep indigo to enrich the black elements of the design.

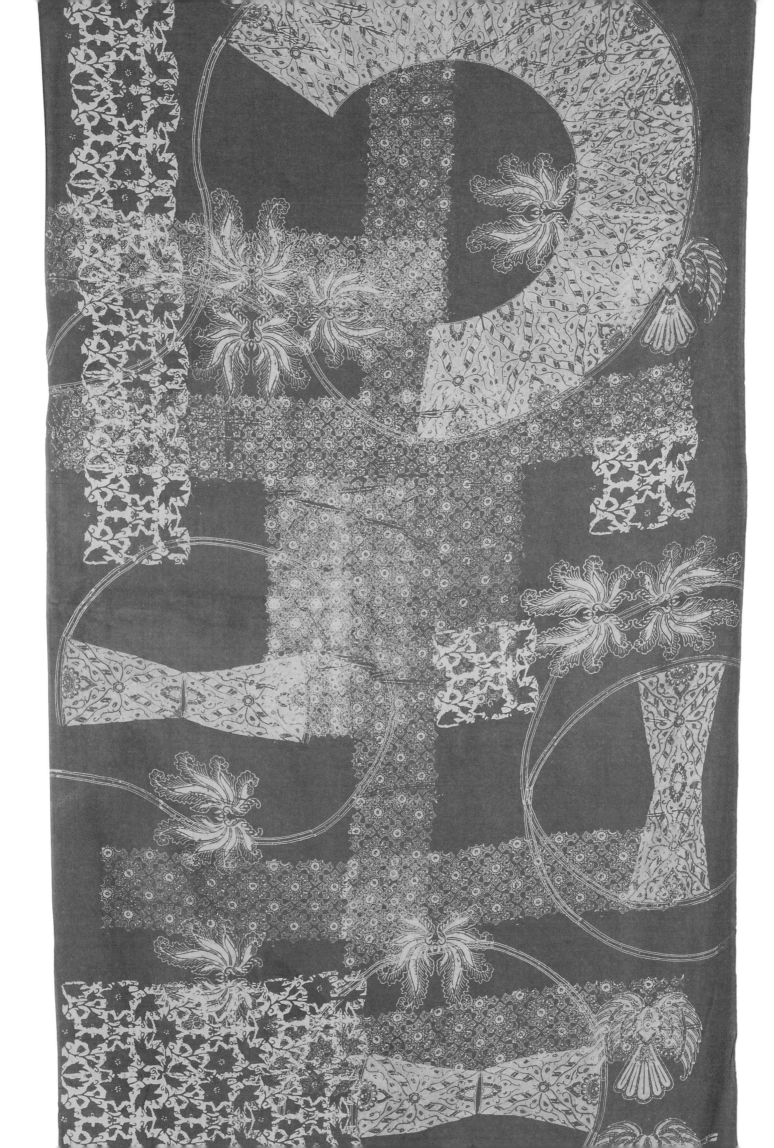

MAKING "HMONG" PILLOW

The Hmong hilltribe in Thailand was once known for cultivating opium poppies, and they inspired the stylized poppy I designed for this pillow. Printing this design requires two blocks (two stamps make each flower). Then it is hand-embroidered with pink and yellow details and a stitched edging. Only some of the many steps involved in making this pillow are pictured here. The design begins on paper, then blocks are carved, printers stamp the pillow, a tailor trims the fabric and sews it to a back panel, and then the pillow is sent to a seamstress for embroidery and edging before it is pressed and packaged. This is how I cultivate opium poppies without getting into trouble!

HAND PAINTING

Pichhwai are Indian religious paintings done in a variety of styles and used to tell stories, including the loose watercolor and the highly refined miniature styles of animals pictured here. On my pillows, you can really see the amazing painted details—a bird's smallest feather and an elephant's ankle bracelet—that sometimes are too small to see in the traditional miniatures. My painter is one of the best in India and will spend up to two whole days making a single pillow.

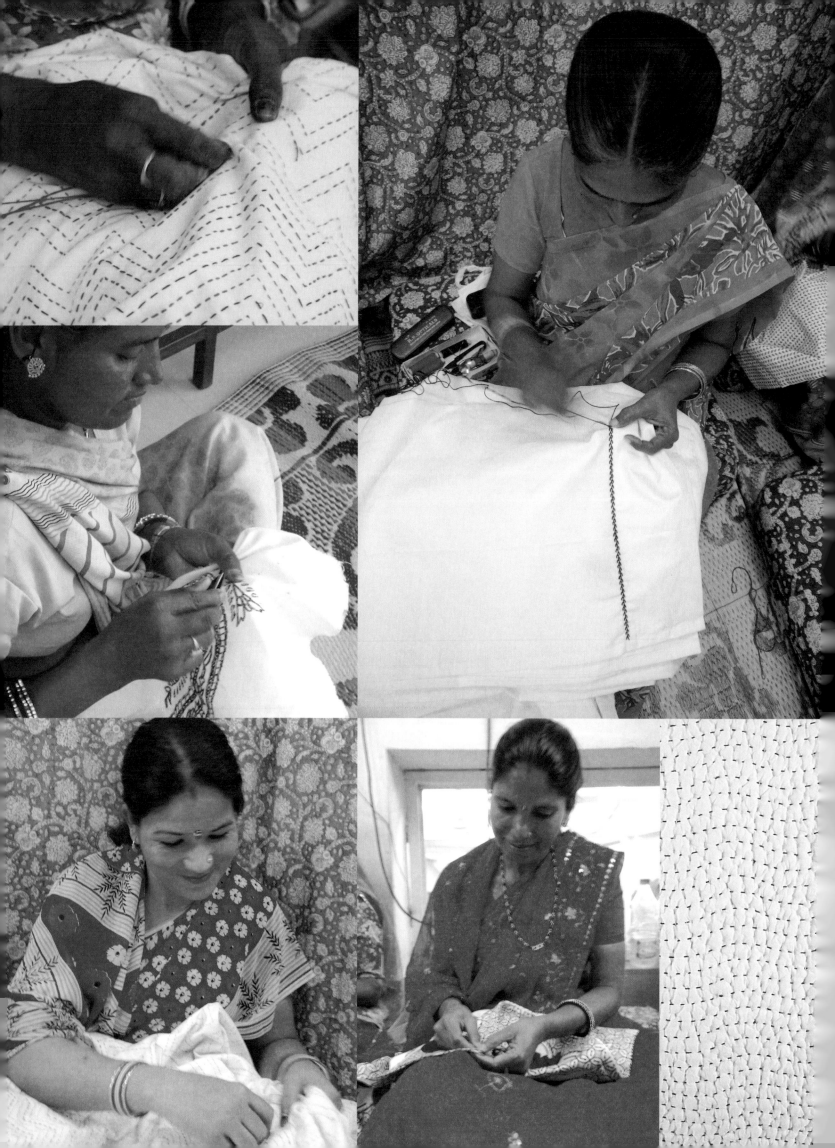

HAND STITCHING

Patient seamstresses hand stitch everything from the edges of sheets and blankets, to the intricate details of pillows and the painstaking patterns on quilts. Hand stitching is of course a tradition in India, passed down from generation to generation. The ladies sew in circles and talk and socialize while they work, which makes it all go faster, since some pieces require an entire day's work to finish.

QUILTING

Before a quilt becomes a quilt, a large yardage of pure cotton voile is hand-printed, then sewn around the edges. Then it is sent to quilters, who will sew the fabric to natural cotton batting by making four-inch squares with double thread stitching. This makes for an incredibly durable quilt. I use the finest cotton voile available, and hand stitch instead of machine stitch, resulting in super-soft quilts that float over your body. You will know you're wrapped up in an Indian-stitched quilt when you don't even notice there are any stitches.

PRINTING DHURRIES

Dhurries, traditional Indian rugs, are usually woven, so my special twist on this classic was to block-print them instead. I use huge, simple blocks saturated with color, sometimes using two or three blocks to complete a design, and they must be pressed extra hard onto the fabric. Then they have to be washed over and over because of the thickness and stiffness of the cotton weave. Together with all the washing, the way the heavy cotton absorbs the color softens the prints around the block's edges, so the dhurries take on an antique, worn look.

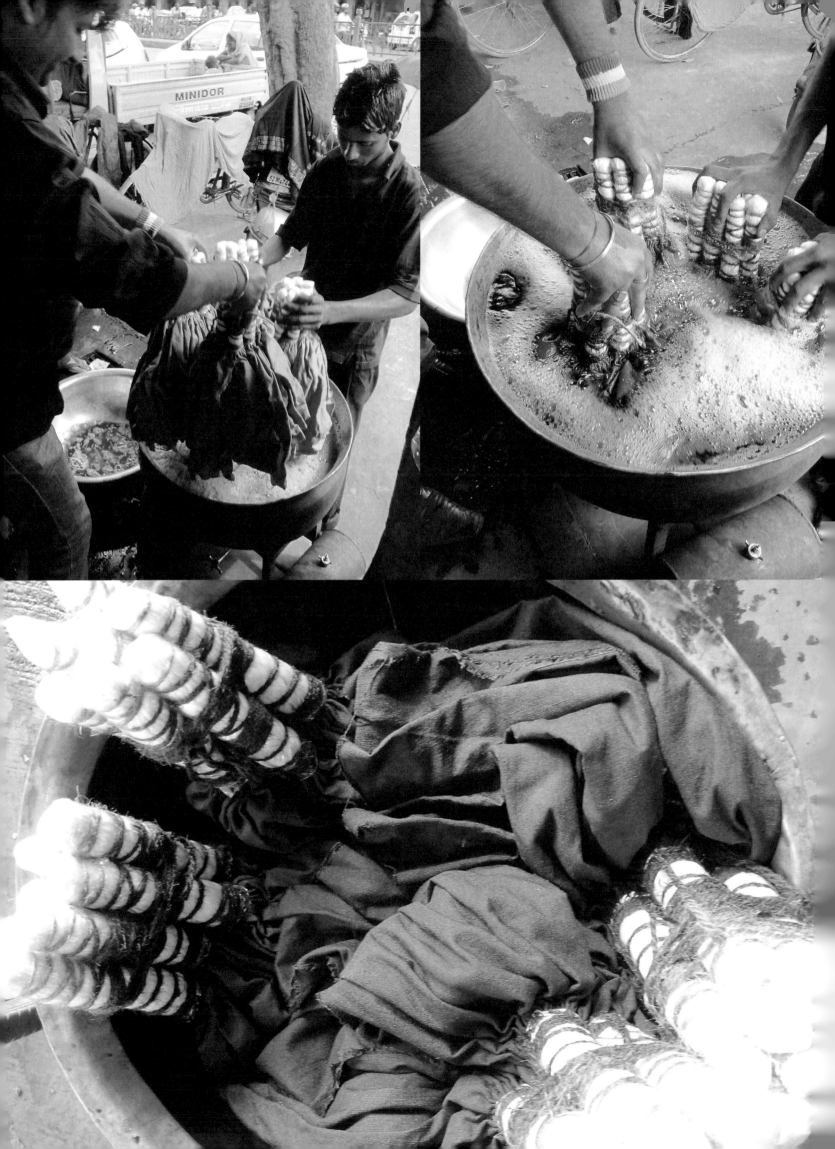

DIPPED PILLOWS

A dipped pillow begins as a linen-cotton swatch of white fabric that gets stitched very tightly at one end, to prevent it from being dyed. The skilled dyers then pull the strings as tightly as they can, cover those ends in heavy plastic, then dip the other halves into vats of hot, water-based dye, sometimes up to fifty times in a row. The more dips, the deeper the pillow's color.

CHURCH DOSSAL

My friend and writer, Elizabeth Garnsey, who is also an Episcopal minister at Church of the Heavenly Rest in New York, told me about liturgical colors, and how they change with each season, and she invited me to create a dossal to hang behind her church's altar for the fifty-day season of Easter. To inspire my ideas she said, "Think of new life, sunrise, rebirth, joy, green plants, spring flowers." When I explained the project to my Hindu partners in India, they smiled and agreed to help me with the printing. For colors I picked local flowers and leaves in Jaipur and gave them to the dye master to match.

The scale of this project was exciting—it turned out to be my Schnabel, of sorts. The panel was so large, it would not fit on the table, so I had to print in sections without a clear idea of how the whole piece would look. Block printing was a fitting method for this piece; the randomness of the stamps is like the uncertainty of life, the hand moving across the fabric and building a whole story one stamp at a time.

BRINGING IT HOME

"What I offer you madame, is a chance to play, to experiment, to learn and most importantly to have a bit of fun at minimal charge."

—A sign spotted in a smooth-talking Indian shopkeeper's window

hen people use my textiles in their homes, I want them to have fun with them and create stories of their own in terms of the way they choose to mix the fabrics all together. I like sharing my adventures, my travels, and my creative process with the interesting people who buy my products. There is no correct way to put it all together. Every bed or living room has the mark of its inhabitants. I hope my textiles bring some spice and adventure into people's lives and living spaces, without any kind of stiff pretense.

I have always created out of a lot of simultaneous ideas, so my products are offshoots of each other, in a way. So even when a bed is covered in a jumble of patterns, stripes, prints, textures, and colors, I think my textiles tend to play well together and relate to each other. These pages illustrate how my textiles can fit together to create surprises in ordinary spaces. A great bed can be its own country, its own land, its own mystery.

In my showroom, I am always adding my finds from the road, and from these, some of my visitors find inspiration for incorporating their own souvenirs and talismans into their living spaces. I brought home matching South Indian canoes, so skinny I don't know who could fit into them to paddle, but they're perfect for pillow displays. I designed a canopy bed covered in hammered sheaths of German silver and thousands of tiny nails, which create their own pattern. (A huge wooden boar peeks out from behind the bed, to inspire me to action!) All over the world I see inlaid tables, some with shells, others with camel bone, and I like how their ancient patterns work next to my modern ones. Nagaland spears and eccentric hats with monkey skulls and boars' tusks protruding at odd angles suggest a native spirit in the room. Headhunters in Nagaland are amazing weavers, and I have collected some impressive examples of their work. Indian miniature paintings and folk paintings always catch my eye for their incredible detail, interesting color palettes, and odd narratives.

At times I have been a bit off with my choices, having taken a left turn when I should have turned right, so to speak. But sometimes a design that didn't work one year makes perfect sense two seasons later, with a whole new bed. I don't plan out design ideas for a room in set patterns. I prefer to keep things unpredictable and a bit risky, so that I remain open to learning and seeing new things. As the saying goes, I like to be out on the skinny branches.

OPPOSITE: I like an informal mixing-up of prints and colors, textures and styles, quite like the way things landed in this room. I designed this German silver bed and had it made in India by carpenters who hammer German silver on top of wood. The silver tarnishes just the right amount. On the bed is one of my tie-dyed quilts, which was hand tied in a way that renders each line irregular and uneven, like an unraveled turban.

My former country house in Connecticut became a repository for my travels of the world. Marching soldiers and oxen and horses storm into the room through this vintage Indian folk painting. My Naga chair and coffee table were made by former headhunters in Nagaland. The hand-printed batik pillows are from Java, and next to the sofa is a tray table by my pal Richard Wrightman, the furniture maker. The turban on the table is one I started making just for fun when I had to go

to a Rajasthan wedding. A Rajasthani's turban is like an American's bow tie; no one can tie their own. So a lot of turbans, like this one, are pre-tied and ready-to-wear. And the saws above the mantle came from a local flea market. I like them for their rustic handmade integrity and their absurd size. How does all this come together? I am forever adding and removing and curating; it's a mobile collection.

Architects on Architecture

Opposite: Indonesian batik pillows fortify my sofa, and a Thai silk sarong on linen hangs over the back. I gave the Moroccan side table a new paint job in gray, so the interesting shape could come forward.

Above, top: I made this corner sofa from a pair of Indian tea house benches—great for storage; their jali fretwork lets you figure out what's inside before having to open them. Thai indigo ikat pillows-as-sofa-back give a soft landing. The Don Quixote etchings on the wall came from a Connecticut flea market.

Bottom left: In India, these blinds are called *Chicks*. They are challenging to order because they're handmade for local markets and difficult to perfectly size to a window. But they do filter just the right amount of light. It reminds me of hot days in India I spent hiding from the sun's intensity. A small patch from an Uzbek textile hangs on the wall, framed in a diagonal stripe, mimicking the sun's rays. On the table, there's a headdress from Zimbabwe, which I have been known to wear at parties.

Bottom right: Sitting on top of an African batik are some old travel guides, which I collect. Sometimes I try to find the old quiet shops they highlight in medieval towns, or I follow the leisurely strolls they politely recommend.

Opposite: The bedroom window panels are made of hand-embroidered saris from Lucknow and hang over an antique iron bed I found in a Connecticut flea market. The poncho from Guatemala above the bed is like a modern drawing, with its deep rich colors and head hole in the middle. I like this corner room for the light that comes in from both sides, lighting up the lavender theme that runs between the quilts, the pouf, and the pillows.

Above top: My mom's old traveling trunk that she inherited from her mother, who used to travel an arduous sixty-mile journey from Manhasset to Baywater, Long Island, when it was a summer house community. I inherited these green walls, and I'm not sure what I think of them, but the textiles do pop against the color. The lamps look like giant drips, and on the bed is one of a few stuffed camels we made from a recycled fabric line.

Above bottom: An early prototype of a Richard Wrightman vintage Chatwin settee, covered in my upholstery fabric. This pair is ideal for a chat with a good pal, since it's sort of like sitting next to someone on a plane.

I made this room for a Peter Dunham *Hollywood at Home* opening. Peter requested many yards of expensive fabric, so, being the thrifty fellow I am, I decided to patch up a wall with prints I already had. The workshop pre-sewed these wall-size panels and sent them over. Peter mixes John Robshaw bedding with collected pieces of his own, including his

Moroccan blanket and a vintage bolster. Poufs in my Ceylon print are on the right. The room pops with the prints, but I wonder if you could ever fall asleep. . . .

Top: The dining room at my house in Kent showcases prints on paper handmade from recycled T-shirt cotton. I make them with old blocks from past collections and random colors printers have left behind—this is how I stay patient in India while waiting around for my workshop to spring into action. The chairs are hand-upholstered with old upholstery fabric made by one of my weekend guests. My guests don't always have to contribute so much, but if they do, they can come anytime!

Bottom left: A vine-covered porch is perfect for summer. Sun filters in through the overgrown vines, while screens keep the bugs at bay. A bright woven dhurrie grounds the table, covered in one of my woven stripe cloths, and dances with the colors of summer picnics. The large print on the dhurrie with the delicate stripe above it creates graphic dimension that makes the space more jolly.

Bottom right: Slippers from Fab India, one of my favorite stops in New Delhi; you never know what you'll find there. These felt oddly Dutch with woven jute on cork treads; here they await tired feet on one of my early woven dhurries.

Opposite: Hand-embroidered blankets from Bengal, such as this one, are a favorite of mine. Stylized flowers and weeds are tossed about with abandon, chaotic and whimsical like a fifth-grader's drawing. In front of it are these more sophisticated, clean, almost modern printed pillows. Together this ensemble is equivalent to the short fat man with the six-foot blonde—they make each other look good.

A fortress of pillows in my New York studio; I like looking at all of my different pillows head on, with the prints, colors, and textures working together and interacting as a massive 3D collage. I get new ideas by combining them in this way. It's like a map of my own personal solar system. *Overleaf:* Snapshot of my office pin board: dye charts for batiks, tantric drawings, paint color

charts; Sadhus to remind me there is a way out of commerce at some point—they look happy in just their dhotis; hand painted swatches of birds; Gandhi to remind me of the big picture; my favorite driver Ashok who absconded with some cash, but I still like him; Bollywood film promotions; Rustem Pasha, my favorite mosque in Istanbul; places I have been, and places I have yet to go.

SELECTIONS FROM JOHN ROBSHAW'S LIBRARY

Barnes, Ruth, Steven Cohen, and Rosemary Crill. *Trade, Temple & Court: The Tapi Collection*. Mumbai: India Book House Ltd., 2003.

Chaldecott, Nada. *Dhurries: History, Pattern, Technique, Identification*. London: Thames & Hudson Ltd., 2003.

Crill, Rosemary, ed. *Textiles from India: The Global Trade*. Calcutta: Seagull Books, 2006.

Fraser-Lu, Sylvia. *Handwoven Textiles of South-east Asia*. London: Oxford University Press, 1988.

Gillow, John. *Traditional Indonesian Textiles*. London: Thames & Hudson Ltd., 1992.

Gillow, John, and Sentance, Bryan. *World Textiles: A Visual Guide to Traditional Techniques*. London: Thames & Hudson Ltd., 1999.

Gittinger, Mattiebelle, ed. *To Speak with Cloth: Studies in Indonesian Textiles*. Los Angeles: Fowler Museum at UCLA, 1989.

Goswamy, B. N. *Indian Costumes in the Collection of the Calico Museum of Textiles*. Ahmedabad, India: Calico Museum of Textiles, 1993.

Hatanaka, Kokyo: *Textile Arts of India*. San Francisco: Chronicle Books, 1996.

Jacobs, Julian. *The Nagas: Hill Peoples of Northeast India*. London: Thames & Hudson Ltd., 1990.

Kossak, Steven. *Indian Court Painting: 16th–19th Century*. London: Thames & Hudson Ltd., 1997.

Mohanty, B. C. , H. D. Naik, and K. V. Chandramouli. *Natural Dyeing Processes of India*. Ahmedabad, India: Calico Museum of Textiles, 1987.

Mookerjee, Ajit, and Madhu Khanna. *The Tantric Way: Art, Science, Ritual*. London: Thames and Hudson Ltd., 1977.

Summerfield, Anne, and John Summerfield. *Walk in Splendor: Ceremonial Dress and the Minangkabau*. Los Angeles: Fowler Museum at UCLA, 1999.

Volwahsen, Andreas. *Imperial Delhi: The British Capital of the Indian Empire*. New York: Prestel, 2002.

TEXTILE MUSEUMS

The Calico Museum of Textiles
Sarabhai Foundation
Opp. Underbridge
Shahibag
Ahmedabad-380 004
Gujarat, India
Tel.: (91) 79 2286 8172
www.calicomuseum.com

Jim Thompson House
6 Soi Kasemsan 2
Rama 1 Road
Bangkok, Thailand
Tel.: (662) 216 7368
www.jimthompsonhouse.com

Musée du Quai Branly
37, quai Branly
75007 Paris, France
Tel.: (33) 01 56 61 70 00
www.quaibranly.fr/en

National Textiles Museum
26, Jalan Sultan Hishamuddin
50050 Kuala Lumpur, Malaysia
Tel.: (606) 3 2694 3457
www.jmm.gov.my/en/museum/national-textiles-museum

The Textile Museum
2320 S. Street, NW
Washington, D.C. 20008-4088
Tel.: (202) 667-0441
www.textilemuseum.org

Siam Society
131 Asoke Montri Road (Sukhumvit 21)
Bangkok, Thailand
Tel.: (66) (0) 2661 64707

www.siam-society.org

INDEX

ACKNOWLEDGMENTS

I would like to acknowledge all of the clever, determined, focused people who have made this book happen in what seemed like a long time, but what in fact was not that long. First, my sprightly editor, Laura Lee Mattingly at Chronicle, who picked up this book midstream as I fought for air; she righted us, pushed us off of the rocks, then firmly directed us downstream. To my graphic design guru and art director, Sarah Caplan, who always has an interesting opinion in times of need and who takes my calls really early in the morning before she feeds her chickens and rides her bike somewhere. To Elizabeth Garnsey, a very distinguished long-time friend who has spirited the writing with panache and wit. To my various friends in India, from Vikram who let me come in and disrupt his workshop just as he was setting it up, to Madhu and Tibbs, who became my partners in India, have been with me from almost the start, and have been great sources of inspiration and energy amidst the chaos of India. To my various photographers who have contributed to this book: Erin Derby, who shoots our catalogs; Hose Cedeno, who has just started shooting for us and is marrying my cousin; Patrick Cline, who did an amazing job of shooting my country house; and Jonas Spinoy, on the ground in India, who has taken my odd ideas for promotional shots and made them happen, with the art direction of Tibbs. To my office of amazing textile junkies for their energy, determination, and zest in covering the world with John Robshaw Textiles. And finally, to all of the craftspeople around the world whom I have worked with, learned from, and simply admired for their incredible designs, traditions, and philosophy on how to live and what is important in life—the pursuit of something real, something made by hand. And, of course, I thank my charming parents and family for all of their support over the years.

—John Robshaw

PHOTOGRAPHY CREDITS